Dead Girl Erased

Table of Contents

Introduction

This project began as a simple idea and became the book in your hands. There were a LOT of steps in between, and a LOT of great poets and writers who stepped outside their comfort zone and jumped into this project.

The idea for this project started in a meeting. Boring, right? Well, when you're ripping pages out of a book, it's not really so boring. I declared to Jennifer (Taylor, Assistant Editor) we would send these pages around the globe and rewrite the book.

We chose to not publicize this open submission call on our website, but only through social media. Over the course of 30 days the responses flooded in.

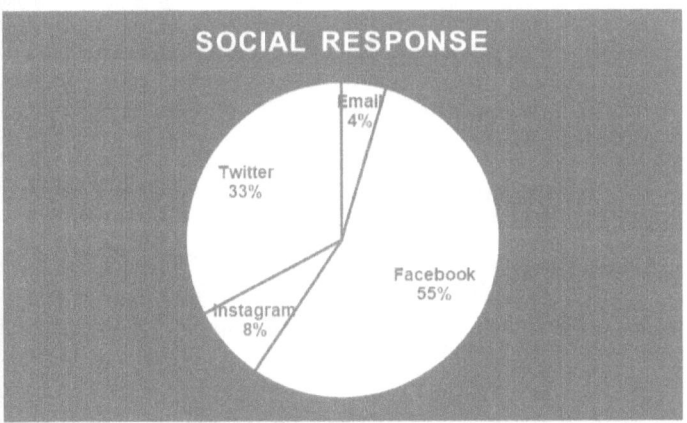

We mailed actual pages ripped from the book to folks all around the world. We included a self-addressed stamped envelope for folks in the US to return, and we asked our overseas friends to pay the postage to return their pages, since we had no idea how the customs and pricing would work.

Outside of the United States, we mailed pages to Canada, Australia, Cyprus, England, Germany, India, Ireland, Luxembourg, Mexico, New Zealand, and the United Kingdom.

We even had one classroom in India participate. We mailed the pages and they never arrived, so we broke our "rules" and scanned in pages for the class to work on. These incredible digital erasure poems are available to view in full color on our website. These high school kids really embraced the challenge and produced some wonderful work. Shout out to their instructor, Shloka Shankar, for incorporating this project into their classroom instruction.

Every day as the mail arrived, I felt like a kid again. With the advent of email, sometimes that personal touch of a mailed letter is lost. Especially exciting were the post-it notes and letter enclosed, fun business cards, quick notes, extra poems on copie paper, and even a grand total of $11. Not all of the pages were returned; but we understand. That's part of doing a project of this undertaking. The unreturned pages are out there waiting to be erased upon their rediscovery.

As this project became more firm and less ethereal, it became apparent there were many poets who had never attempted erasure poetry before. Some had never heard of this style of poem. The second part of this project was born. There is now a 3" 3-ring binder which houses all of the original pages along with all the ephemera received. The binder will be available on loan to organizations and instructors who are teaching erasure poetry.

I don't want to ruin the surprise inside, but you will find gorgeous illustrations, sewn blackout, permanent marker erasures, pencil and pen drawings and marks, and even added stickers and tape. Unfortunately, this book doesn't do justice to the tactile sensation of some of these poems. We tried our bes to present the work as authentically as possible.

inally, a huge shout out to our constant supporters who
embraced this project and shared the word with friends and
other poets who participated.

We hope you try your hand at erasure poetry. There are some
wonderful books by single authors, of single works erased, and
of a variety of methods. Don't be constrained in your creative
endeavors! Keep pushing those boundaries.

Enjoy *Dead Girl Erased.*

Karen Cline-Tardiff
Editor-in-Chief

1

Washington State's Pacific Coast
Yearning Sands Resort
September of last year

Before Priscilla Carter came to Yearning Sands to be the resort's assistant manager, she supposed her life here would involve a blend of poetry, nature and wealth. She imagined long walks among the towering pines, evenings spent in the luxurious lobby, sipping a cocktail while watching the sun set across the restless Pacific, and a wealthy, interesting man who would catch sight of her and rush to her side, drawn by the rhapsody of their souls.

That hadn't happened.

When a wealthy, interesting man did show up——and they did, on a regular basis, because Yearning Sands was a destination resort——he was usually married to someone smart, pretty and young. If a single guy caught her gazing at the sunset, he would inevitably tell her his room needed to be cleaned. Her two seemingly good prospects bought her a couple of drinks, gave her a quick grope and rushed for the finish line, and when she demanded romance and promises, they couldn't be bothered. Every viable candidate treated her as if she was a slave, and not the kind they wanted to handcuff and spank and have wild sex with, either. More like a faceless vehicle who lived to make their lives easier. That was *so* not her.

The man she considered her best prospect, actor Carson Lennex, had reported her brazen behavior to the resort owners. In forceful terms, Mr. Di Luca had reminded Priscilla that her role here was to assist Mrs. Di Luca, the resort's manager. He'd used words like *probation* and *trial period* and suggested she might consider chasing her dreams elsewhere.

Elsewhere? She didn't have another position—or a runaway marriage—lined up. So she went to work and got her chores done…mostly.

Priscilla was in training to take over from Annie Di Luca when Annie had one of her sick spells—Annie was *really old* and suffered from rheumatoid arthritis—or when the Di Lucas went on one of their rare vacations.

The main hotel building resembled a European castle with towers and turrets, and 592 rooms. Forty-eight cottages were scattered around the property. The resort hosted whale-watching tours and fishing expeditions off their dock, hiking trips to the nearby Olympic Mountains and expertly led scientific treks seeking local flora and fauna. They rented all-terrain vehicles, bicycles and small launches. They had four bars, twenty-seven miles of running paths and a beach access that led to the second-longest beach in Washington State. Luxury-inclined guests indulged in the infinity pool, the fine the wind called Belated . In the moonless night, She only knew to place a

darkness curiosity, and wine, . She found a hole For its size, it was heavy; in her chest, present.

She stared and wondered what was, So valuable

nothing

but hope

inside

the figure of a man

startled

with glaring eyes and ferocious scowls.

sneaking around wet and dirty

"whispered.

whoever would be doubly cursed.

crumpled in death's agony,

back.

back.

back.

fear.

back Now.

run away.

that box of cursed statues

used

pushed

out

face snatched

had

she had nowhere to go

no desire

isolation

everything

loved left her

that dark, cold

followed her She

pared to fly

climbed

through the rain toward the

black

the other side

CUT, BROWN EYES, WHEELCHAIR BOUND. RHEU-
MATOID ARTHRITIS. RESORT MANAGER. BRIL-
LIANT WITH STAFF AND GUESTS. KIND TO A FAULT.
FRAIL. HUSBAND: NAPOLEONE (LEO) DILUCA,
MARRIED "SINCE THE EARTH'S CRUST COOLED."

"We'll be back in two weeks," Annie said. "After
my last experience with an assistant, I was determined
not to hire a replacement. But Leo insisted, and you
know the only reason I relented was because you were
a wounded veteran."

"I wasn't that wounded." Kellen rotated her shoulder.

"Enough that the Army discharged you!"

"Men were killed." *I was unconscious for two days.
Had an MRI to discover the cause of my coma. Tricky
things, land mines. Woke to find myself being dis-
charged; I hadn't realized the military could process
paperwork that fast.*

"I'm sorry, dear, about the deaths. I know how you
feel about your comrades in arms."

They reached the car where Mitchell Nyugen waited
to drive the DiLucas to the airstrip. Again her mind
spun and Mitch's info popped up, like a little index card:

MITCHELL NYUGEN:
MALE. VIETNAMESE AMERICAN, SECOND GEN-
ERATION, 26, 5'9", 160 LBS., EXCELLENT PHYSI-
CAL CONDITION, NEEDS LITTLE SLEEP. NO
AFFECTIONATE ATTACHMENTS. ARMY VETERAN,
HONORABLE DISCHARGE. EXPERT LICENSED
DRIVER—MILITARY VEHICLES & COMMERCIAL
DRIVER'S LICENSE (CDL) (TRACTOR TRAILER).

EMPLOYED 79 DAYS. DRIVER, MECHANIC, ELECTRONICS. FRIEND.

Mitch was one of Kellen's men. Skilled woodworkers, electricians, maintenance and handy workers didn't have to come to Washington in the wettest, darkest, most miserable time of the year, so when Annie appealed to Kellen for a chauffeur, Kellen had in turn appealed to Mitch. Mitch, who had been driving long hours for a trucking company, leaped at the chance to work at the resort.

He was the first of her people to arrive at Yearning Sands.

Now he opened the door and Hammett hopped onto his cushion on the floor. Mitch dried the dog, then picked Annie up and deposited her on the seat.

"Thank you, Mitch. When Leo comes out, will you help him with the bags?" she asked.

"Of course, Mrs. Di Luca." Mitch backed out of the car.

"That boy is so formal," Annie said to Kellen. "I've told him to call me Annie, and he won't."

"He's from the South. Houston. Things are more formal there. He still calls me captain."

"Half of the staff call you captain." Annie patted the seat. "Won't you come in and sit for a minute?"

Kellen shed her rain poncho and handed Mitch the umbrella before easing inside. She took a second towel and dried Hammett some more, then scratched him under the chin. As she stroked his soft head, the anxiety she felt about taking charge of the resort faded.

Mitch shut the door, encasing the two in quiet leather

Dead Girl Running 29a
Stan Galloway

I know warm
shoulders. You feel
a fever, my darling,
our overnight rolling behind,
the staff
stubborn,
like raised eyebrows
standing out in
creaky bones, cheek
kissed   warm   fun
a riotous good time.
I was coming,
do you remember?
Do you feel as if you
spun like a top on the far
edge of
fear,
black hole that swallowed every day,
released an honorable position that would fit:
unique
        united
                yearning.

Cecilia a
good wife. I understand what he wants"

He should understand you."

Her ribs hurt
hurt where he had kicked her.
. He, disciplines me when I need it."
When do you need it?

couldn't contain her outrage.

you weren't
expected to live?"

"I'm lucky he chose me.
They're wealthy, influential. wind
blew hard, blew her own
words back in her face

They're so self-
important

Feeble excuse. it was all Cecilia
had,

we can be   *children*

tired of

standing in

corners

Look at

the beauti-
ful

gold   *Now*

A

terra-cotta
ghost

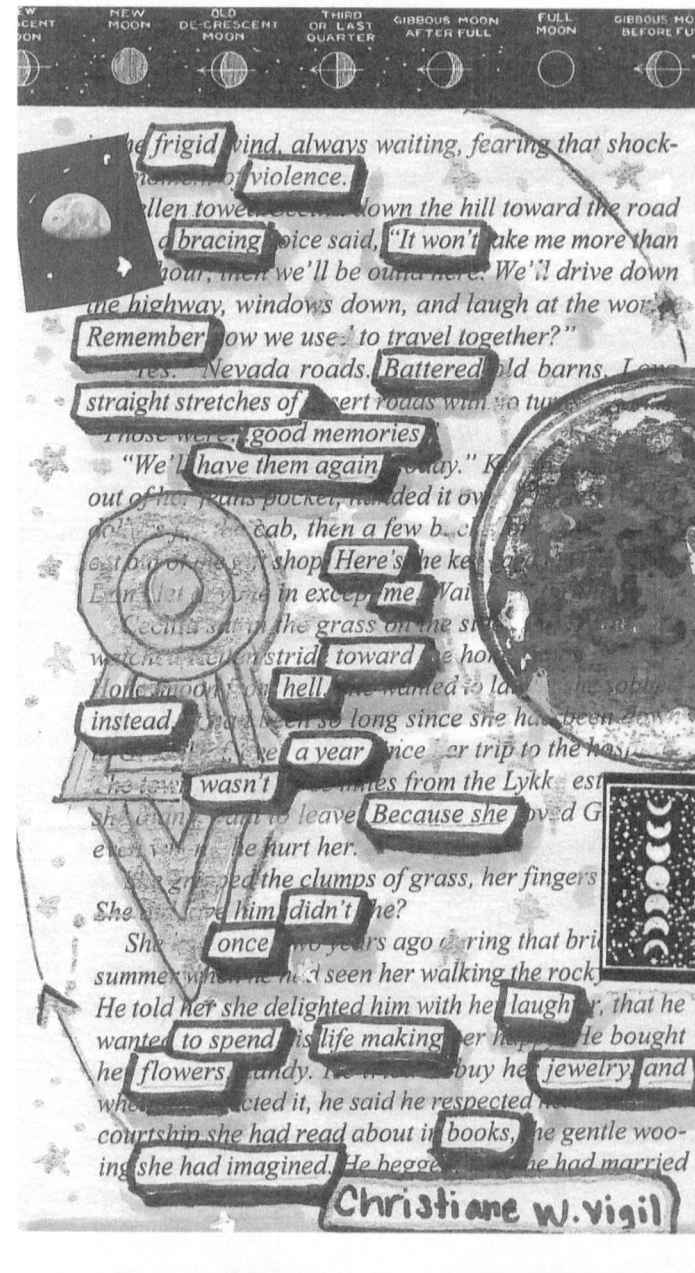

e frigid wind, always waiting, fearing that shock-
moment of violence.

llen towe down the hill toward the road
a bracing oice said, "It won't ake me more than
hour, then we'll be outta here. We'll drive down
the highway, windows down, and laugh at the wor
Remember how we used to travel together?"

Yes. Nevada roads. Battered old barns. Lo
straight stretches of sert roads with no tu
Those were good memories.

"We'll have them again today." K
out of her jeans pocket, handed it ov
do e cab, then a few b c
e bag of the gift shop Here's the ke
I am let nyone in except me. Wai
Cecilia sat in the grass on the si
watched e en stride toward e hor
Honeymoon hell. She wanted to la he sobb
instead. na been so long since she has been
a year ince er trip to the ho
e to wasn't es from the Lykk est
she d n ant to leave Because she ov d G
e y hurt her.
gr ed the clumps of grass, her fingers
She love him didn't e?
She once two years ago ring that bri
summer when he had seen her walking the rock
He told her she delighted him with her laugh r, that he
wanted to spend is life making er ha e bought
her flowers andy. e buy he jewelry and
wh cted it, he said he respected
courtship she had read about in books, e gentle woo-
ing she had imagined. He begge e had married

Christiane W. Vigil

God,

said

think

what

cruelties

man,

reached

In ███ the ███████████████ drawer
███ they kept ██ light██ for the fire.
██ kill you and ██ kill ████
████ what ████ ended. ██t he ████ killed ██
████████████ now—
He █licked the ██████████████
flame.
████████ d██ew ██ gaze ██████ out the window.
He saw ██████████ her█ H█ooked ████
██ body. Looked █ again, ██ face twisted ██ to█
████ fury.
█he ████ exploded.

Don't mind the
Stain...
its just a
Toblerone bar

4

"Captain? You okay? ~~It's really~~ rainin' ~~out here. You want to come inside?~~"

~~At the sound of Russell's voice, Kellen shed the~~ grim ~~memories like rainwater. She looked at the man who stood~~ outside ~~the portico, holding an umbrella over her and staring anxiously.~~

~~RUSSELL CLARK:~~
~~MALE, 46, 5'11", 220 LBS., AUTISTIC. YEARNING SANDS DOORMAN SINCE HE WAS 16. GOOD AT HIS JOB. WILL NOT GO ON VACATION EVEN IN WINTER. LIKES/NEEDS ROUTINE.~~

She looked down at ~~herself, at the yellow plastic rain poncho that draped her to~~ her knees ~~and protected her from~~ the worst ~~of the rain, and at the~~ soggy ~~hem of her long black dress and the damp~~ leather ~~of her fashion boots.~~

~~She~~ mentally checked her schedule, ~~made sure she had her top security I'm-the-acting manager~~ pass ~~card~~

EMPLOY

FEAR

know how to

choose

to

confronta

The ... killer's mind.

"I can't wait to see what they concoct." With a nod to them both, he strode toward his private elevator.

Kellen realized she had been holding her breath. She let it out slowly. "He's never spoken to me directly before."

"Don't let it give you ideas," Sheri Jean snapped. "The last assistant manager got reprimanded for thinking she would make him a good trophy wife."

"Sheri Jean, do you see this?" Kellen circled her own unsmiling face. "This saw combat in Afghanistan and Kuwait. This has no illusions left, and you do not comprehend what you're challenging."

Sheri Jean took a step back.

Kellen continued, "In fifteen minutes, I'm scheduled to speak to Chef Norbert about tonight's menu and I know he, also, will be testing my fitness to run the resort in Annie's absence. After that, I speak to Chef Reinhart, who will be irritated that I spoke to Chef Norbert first. Both of those gentlemen will also have to be reminded that after several tours into the world's war zones, I was wounded and then honorably discharged from the US Army as a captain, and I am fit to lead this resort."

Sheri Jean's mouth opened, then closed without a word.

"It's a good thing we're currently running only a skeleton crew. If I had to repeat that too often, I would grow irritated. I'll see you at two fifteen." With military precision, Kellen turned back to the view and waited while Sheri Jean's heels clicked away across the tile.

The men and women Kellen had led could have warned Sheri Jean not to challenge Kellen's authority. In Afghanistan, in her first deployment, superior officers and soldiers had taken one look at her and assumed she would be a pushover. They hadn't realized how fiercely she would push back, and why.

She would never be abused again.

When Annie had interviewed her for this position and asked about Kellen's goal, her answer had been "A home." But it wasn't as simple as that. The deaths of her parents had left Cecilia orphaned at nine. Her aunt and uncle had taken her in and given her stability, but they weren't her own mother and father. Only Cousin Kellen had made her feel a true part of the family with wholehearted generosity of spirit.

Then Gregory happened; he had successfully dug into her psyche and undermined her strengths. Looking back, she recognized that and knew, too, that Cousin Kellen had saved her; Cousin Kellen had died for her. So that was what *this* Kellen wanted, to find a place in this world where she could be safe, where she could bring her friends, raise them up and give them security. She wanted to be to her friends what Cousin Kellen had been to her: the person who had the strength to make the world better, the person who created a safe haven for lost souls…like herself.

With two minutes to spare, Kellen strode into the restaurant kitchens. The two chefs' hulking forms stood opposite one another.

CHEF NORBERT/CHEF REINHART:
BROTHERS, 47 AND 46. WHITE, BOTH 6'5", 240 LBS., BLOND, BLUE EYES, VIRILE, IMPOSING. RECENTLY IMMIGRATED FROM GERMANY. MASTER CHEFS. FIVE-STAR FOOD IN TWO RESTAURANTS. LOUD. ARROGANT. *RIVALS.*

r time
was irritated,
pacing and   flailing.

The   between
minutes.

a

contract

Withi   t her temper

she went   waiting
immaculate, a

a   fountain.

What is ██████████████ *a mountain* ████████?

██████ *that* ████ *gleam* ██████

"██████████████████,"

"██████████████ changed!"

██████████████
██████████████. She stood ██████
████████████ in agony.

"██████████████████████
"██████████████ She couldn't ██████
██████ be ██ ... ██████████████
██████████████
██████████████ open ██████
██████ to ████████████, prove
██████

██████ It didn't make sense. ██████
██████████████
██████ the pain ██████
██████ advised her ██████
██████████████ program ██████

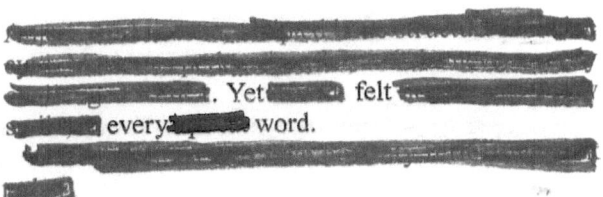

. Yet ▬▬ felt ▬▬ every ▬▬ word.

sented us with a challenge." He picked up a pair of binoculars from the windowsill and handed them to Kellen.

Through the veil of rain, in the distance, two coyotes fought over a bone while vultures dived and scolded. Kellen texted Temo: "Someone in maintenance will go out and pick up the skeleton."

Mara took the binoculars and looked, too. "Do you know how upset guests get when they see scavengers cleaning up a dead deer or a raccoon or whatever?"

"Some people are not meant to appreciate the fullness of a natural life." Xander spread his fingers above Kellen's shoulder and let them hover there. "You're in pain. I have time on my schedule for a massage."

"Thank you, Xander, but I've got another couple of appointments, then I need to see where we are on orders and bookings."

"You will have time later for a run, won't you?" Mara asked. "Not far—we'll race each other back to our cottages."

"You'll win," Kellen said. "My cottage is the last one."

Mara smiled brightly. "I know!"

Xander's hands settled over Kellen's SC joint and massaged. "Something long denied is fighting to erupt from your spiritual center and to ignore it would have dire results on not only your well-being, and the well-being of the resort, which you now lead."

Kellen questioned Mara with wide eyes and a pursed mouth.

"Better go for a quick massage," Mara said. "Last time he said something like that, Destiny spilled a bottle of lavender massage oil on the rug and we had to have it cleaned twice before it stopped exuding inappropriate amounts of serenity into the air."

I DO

He didn't deserve to have her

She checked her texts.

Nothing

soon, she'd give him a call

her head

a crypt. She stepped over the line.

a woman crying   headed out to
a   fight.

furious

MALE,
6'1" 145 LBS

FORMAL CLOTHING

BACKGROUND   UNKNOWN

Today he wore a black turtleneck

rules.

devastate her

her brain snapped

's blue ▮▮▮ and black s▮▮▮▮▮, ▮▮▮▮▮▮▮ keys in her hand. W▮▮▮▮▮▮▮▮▮▮▮▮▮▮, ▮▮▮▮▮▮▮▮▮▮▮ ▮▮ h▮▮ ▮▮▮▮▮▮▮▮▮▮▮▮▮▮▮▮▮▮▮▮▮▮ the ▮▮ests.

"▮▮▮▮▮▮▮▮▮▮▮▮▮▮▮▮▮▮▮▮▮▮▮▮?"

"▮▮▮▮▮▮▮▮▮▮▮▮▮▮ appropriate ▮▮▮▮▮ for welcoming guests, K▮▮▮▮▮▮▮▮▮ ▮▮▮ she ▮▮▮▮▮▮▮▮▮▮.

▮▮▮o was gone. M▮▮▮▮▮▮▮▮▮▮▮▮▮▮▮▮▮▮▮▮▮▮▮ ▮▮▮▮▮▮▮▮▮▮▮▮▮▮▮▮▮▮▮▮▮▮▮▮▮▮▮▮▮▮▮▮▮ ▮▮▮▮▮▮▮▮▮▮▮ appropriate ▮▮▮▮▮▮▮▮▮▮▮.

▮▮▮▮▮▮▮▮▮▮▮▮▮▮▮▮▮▮▮▮▮▮▮▮▮▮▮; i▮ ▮▮▮ ▮▮▮▮▮ ▮▮▮▮▮ everyone was either on vacation ▮▮ trying to cover for everyone else. S▮▮ ▮▮▮▮▮▮▮ "Only if I ▮▮▮▮▮▮▮▮.

"Feeling ▮▮▮▮ f▮▮▮▮▮ 1?" ▮▮▮▮▮ asked.

"▮▮▮▮▮▮▮▮▮▮▮▮." D▮▮▮▮▮▮▮ ▮▮▮▮▮▮▮▮ ▮▮▮▮▮▮▮▮▮ ▮▮▮▮▮ ▮▮▮▮ her c▮▮▮▮▮▮▮▮▮ ▮▮▮▮▮▮▮, ▮▮▮▮▮▮▮, ▮▮▮▮▮▮▮▮ ▮▮▮ ▮ ▮▮▮▮▮▮▮ of ▮▮▮▮▮ "D▮ you ▮▮▮ ▮▮▮ l▮▮▮▮▮▮▮▮?"

"I ordered them. You get them from the kitchen. I'll b▮▮▮▮ ▮▮▮▮▮▮."

"G▮▮▮▮▮▮▮▮▮▮▮ ▮▮▮▮▮ I'll change a▮▮ ▮▮▮▮▮ you ▮▮ the k▮▮▮▮▮ ▮▮▮▮." S▮▮ ▮▮▮▮▮▮▮▮ ▮▮▮ TV ▮▮ ▮▮▮▮ ▮▮▮▮ ▮▮▮▮d her ▮▮▮▮▮▮ ▮▮ the farthest c▮▮▮▮▮ of ▮▮▮ ▮▮▮▮'s p▮▮▮▮▮. S▮▮ ▮▮▮ ▮▮ ▮▮▮▮ ▮▮ ▮▮▮ idea t▮ ▮▮▮▮ h▮▮ ▮▮▮▮ ▮▮▮▮ newly arrived g▮▮▮▮. I ▮▮▮ ▮▮▮ ▮▮ the ▮▮▮▮ ▮▮ ▮▮▮ tired, h▮▮▮▮▮ ▮▮▮ ▮▮▮▮▮, ▮▮▮ ▮ ▮▮▮▮pt ▮▮▮▮▮▮▮▮ of s▮▮▮▮▮ ▮▮▮▮▮, ▮▮▮ ▮▮▮▮ ▮▮▮▮ ▮▮▮ ▮▮▮ cr▮▮▮, and pros▮▮▮▮▮ wrapped artichokes never failed to ▮▮▮ ▮▮▮ ▮▮ ▮▮▮ ▮▮▮▮▮▮. K▮▮▮▮'▮ ▮▮▮▮▮▮ ▮▮▮▮▮ s▮▮▮▮▮▮▮ul strategy, a pain in the ▮▮▮ ▮▮▮ successful.

▮▮▮ her c▮▮▮▮▮▮, ▮▮▮ j▮▮▮▮▮ ▮▮▮▮ h▮▮ ▮▮▮▮▮▮▮▮▮ costume: l▮▮▮ ▮▮▮▮▮▮▮, ▮ ▮▮▮▮▮▮ ▮▮▮▮▮ button-up shirt and

of duty, ambushed outside their home. He had died in
her arms.

"How's it going?" Kellen asked gently. "Parents talk-
ing to you yet?"

"On the phone. My ... my dad and my mothe ...
Birdie's parents and ... widow to take a job so ... for
work when her hu ... troit hadn't improved ... do what
she'd been tra.... mi ... ber at night. ... eternal love. ...
pain tainted ... ves had never ... had watched ...

NIXIE   911   CC

RETURN TO
ATTEMPTED –
UNABLE TO

BC: 78362005858

7203/25/23

SENDER
NOT KNOWN
FORWARD

*0488-16189-16-42

*The gas explosion sent a blast at Cecilia that lifted
her, then slammed her into the ground. She lost con-
sciousness, then came back, panicked. She smelled
burning cloth. Burning flesh. Sweet Jesus, smoke
drifted past her face.*

*Someone threw a coat over her head, blinding her,
panicking her.*

She fought.

*Suddenly she was free. Her ears were roaring with
some...sound.*

*A man leaned into her line of vision. He was shout-
ing at her, gesturing toward his own head, then hers.
She read his lips. "Lady, your hair was on fire!" She
turned her head away from the direction of the house,*

The cops!"

lights flashing, a fire engine

Cecilia flinched. Yes, she could escape

the explosion

the road

sick.

burned all over.

Her lips
cracked. The heat,

empty of everyone

Kellen's key.

burned away.

When you're ready,

Realization *Of course*
In the
trivia of
God.
a command,

of *curiosity and*

condition.
see a doctor as soon as possible."

you. *limped* *, pushed*
the doors
faced front,
collapsed against the railing

signs *moved*

narrow, old-fashioned

the wail of
movement.

. She shrugged
and stripped.

By: Lauren Castorena

bra. Gregory had insisted she wear one. For decency, he said. So men wouldn't stare at her. What men? He never allowed her around other men. To hell with him.

She eased her wedding ring off her finger, his grandmother's wedding ring, and stared at the blisters raised by the heated platinum. Even his family wedding ring had burned her. Yes! To hell with Gregory. She flung the ring into the trash can.

Willy-nilly, she chose an outfit from Kellen's wardrobe. She sat on the bed to pull on the jeans. When she stood, they slipped off her skinny hips. She had to notch Kellen's belt on the last hole and it was barely enough to keep the pants up.

More sirens.

Panicked, she ran into the bathroom for the toiletries. She flipped on the light and— No wonder everyone stared and wanted her to go to the hospital. She put her hands to her head. Strands of hair cracked off in her hands. She rubbed her face. Her eyebrows...gone, burned off by the blast. Her skin looked thin, mottled, as if the explosion had slapped her. Her blue eyes...were haunted.

Leaning over the sink, she used Kellen's brush and gingerly brushed what was left of her hair. In Kellen's overnight bag, she found a pair of scissors and cut off the random long strands. Now she looked like a Halloween monster in June. But not so wounded, more like a fashion statement gone bad.

In the bedroom, she tossed the toiletries into the suitcase. She swooped down to get two pairs of shoes off the closet floor—and came face-to-face with the locked room safe. She froze. She had no money. Like the key, the money had disappeared with her pocket. She sank to her knees. She needed what was in that safe. But she had no way in. She couldn't break into a safe...

Wait. Maybe she didn't have to break in. Aunt Cora Rae and Uncle Earle had always used the same password for everything. ECKC. Earle, Cora, Kellen, Cecilia. 3, 2, 5, 2. The family knew the code. Maybe Kellen had used the code.

With shaking fingers, Cecilia pressed 3, 2, 5, 3. Nothing happened.

She dropped her head into her hands. What other code would Kellen use? Maybe her girlfriend's name... but she didn't know it. If Cecilia and Kellen had been able to drive away from Greenleaf, roll down the windows, let the wind blow their hair...then she would have known. She would have rejoiced in their relationship. Instead, Cecilia was grief-stricken, and Kellen's girlfriend remained a mystery.

Desperate, Cecilia punched in the same code. 3, 2, 5...2.

The safe sang a little song and the door opened. She'd done it wrong the first time.

Gregory's voice sang in her head. You're incompetent. You're not fit to be out on your own.

"Shut up." Inside, she found Kellen's credit card, five neatly folded twenties, a black velvet box with a blue enamel wedding band inside... Cecilia stared at that band. Kellen had wanted to marry her girlfriend, and...the young woman Kellen loved would suffer a loss she would never comprehend. With a snap, Cecilia shut the box and placed it in a side pocket of the suitcase.

At the bottom of the safe, she found Kellen's computer. She smoothed her hand across the black matte finish. She hadn't been allowed to touch a computer

▓▓▓▓▓▓▓▓▓▓▓▓▓▓▓▓▓▓▓▓ *discover,* ▓▓▓▓▓▓▓
▓▓▓▓▓▓▓▓▓▓▓ *the* ▓▓▓▓▓▓▓▓▓▓▓▓▓▓▓▓
▓▓▓▓▓▓▓▓▓▓▓▓▓▓▓▓▓▓▓▓ *dead.* ▓▓▓▓
▓▓▓▓▓▓▓▓▓▓▓▓▓▓▓▓▓▓▓▓▓▓▓▓▓▓
▓▓▓▓▓▓▓▓▓▓▓▓▓▓▓▓▓▓ *life* ▓▓▓▓
▓▓▓▓▓▓▓▓▓▓▓

▓▓▓▓▓▓▓▓▓▓▓▓▓ *on the bed.* ▓▓▓▓▓▓
▓▓▓▓▓▓▓▓▓▓▓▓▓▓▓▓▓▓▓▓▓▓▓▓
l bras ▓▓▓▓▓▓▓▓▓▓▓▓▓▓▓▓▓▓▓▓
▓▓▓▓▓▓▓▓▓▓▓▓▓▓▓▓▓▓▓▓▓▓▓
▓▓ *Somehow,* ▓▓▓▓▓▓▓▓▓▓▓▓▓▓
▓▓▓▓▓▓▓▓▓▓▓▓▓▓▓▓▓▓

▓▓▓▓▓▓▓ *bulged;* ▓▓▓▓▓▓▓▓▓▓▓▓
▓▓ *She* ▓▓▓▓▓▓▓▓▓▓▓▓▓▓▓▓▓▓▓▓
▓▓▓▓▓▓▓▓▓▓▓▓▓▓▓▓▓▓▓▓▓▓▓
▓▓▓▓▓▓▓▓ *pushed the button* ▓▓▓▓▓▓▓
▓▓▓▓▓▓▓▓▓▓▓▓▓▓▓▓▓▓▓▓
▓▓▓▓▓▓▓▓▓▓▓▓▓▓▓▓
fast ▓▓▓ *a Mini* ▓▓▓▓▓▓▓▓▓▓▓▓▓▓▓
▓▓▓▓▓▓▓▓▓▓▓▓▓▓▓▓▓▓▓▓▓
▓▓▓▓ *suitcase,* ▓▓▓▓▓▓▓▓▓▓▓▓▓▓
screamed, ▓▓▓▓▓▓▓▓▓▓▓▓▓▓▓▓▓
▓▓▓▓▓▓▓▓▓▓▓▓▓▓▓▓▓▓

▓▓▓▓▓▓▓▓▓▓▓▓▓▓▓▓▓▓▓▓
▓▓▓▓▓▓▓▓ *Panic* ▓▓▓▓▓▓▓▓▓▓▓▓
▓▓ *fast,* ▓▓▓▓▓▓▓▓▓▓▓▓▓▓▓▓▓▓
▓▓▓ *Drive* ▓▓▓▓▓▓▓▓▓▓▓▓▓▓▓
▓▓▓▓▓▓▓▓▓▓ *without looking* ▓▓▓▓▓▓
▓▓▓▓▓▓▓▓▓▓▓▓▓▓ *south.* ▓▓▓▓
▓▓▓▓▓▓ *she was going.* ▓▓▓▓▓▓▓▓▓▓
▓▓▓▓▓▓▓▓▓▓ *she would never return* ▓▓▓▓

were convinced

convinced
that anyone could survive
walking and talking.

, outbursts of laughter.

find an exit wound.

a person
a whole year
memories

thoughtfully
shot
Pause. Pause.

too much
waiting
nothing
oh God!–
to be dealt
their breath.

there ██████████ doing the most ███████████
████████ until █████████ he mortars started rain-
ing down. ████████████████████ suddenly there
████████ seconds in a minute. ████████████
█████████████ the atmosphere was █████
parable.

███████████████████████████████████
███████████████████████████████████

██████████ speculation ████████████ creeps.
████████ caught █████████████████
██████ and turned ████████████████████
██████████ in ████ despair, ██████████

Too close. ██████████████ wealthy lover ███████
███████████████████████████████
███████████████████████████████
███████████████████ a quavering breath. ███
████████ talk to me again. ████ meet my eyes ████
forget ████████████████████████

███████████████████████████████████
███████████████████████████████████
███████████████████████████████████
Damn it. ████████████████████████████
███████████████ do it ████████████
██████████ It couldn't hurt. ████████████
███████████████████████████████████

██████████ a bright smile ████████████████
███████████████████████████████████
just dropped out of the clouds. ████████████

EARLY 70S. ANNUALLY VISIT YEARNING SANDS
FOR MYSTERY WEEKEND.

NILS BROOKS:
MALE, 30S, 6', 180 LBS. DARK-RIMMED GLASSES.
CUTE. NERDY.

Kellen didn't recognize anybody and nobody appeared to recognize her. She relaxed a previously unnoticed tension in her shoulders. She'd been thinking too much about Greenleaf, making herself jumpy. Because Xander had told her to, she breathed, and because she was in the hospitality business, she smiled.

Birdie continued, "We'll be transporting you to the resort. We've parked the van at the end of the stairs. As you can imagine, in this weather, our goal is to keep you as dry as possible."

Some chuckles.

"It's too windy for umbrellas, but if you need a poncho, I have them. One size fits all!" Birdie raised the yellow plastic over her head. "But first, Kellen has some hors d'oeuvres to sustain you until you get to the resort. Help yourselves to one on the way out the door, and don't worry — we have more in the van."

The promise of treats got the group moving in a hurry. Everyone took one, descended the steps, gasped at the lash of the wind and rain and headed for the van.

Out of the corner of her mouth, Birdie asked, "Are those two old enough to be married?"

Kellen knew exactly what she meant.

Justin and Julia held hands and smiled at each other. When the ladies from Alaska asked about their love story, the two of them gushed that they'd met as freshmen at Wenatchee Valley College, dated until they both graduated, and gotten married in January because it was the cheapest time of the year.

The pilot unloaded the luggage onto a cart and pushed it toward the back of the van; when Birdie started to lift the suitcases, Justin leaped forward and took over. Nice kid. Julia waited patiently, then the newlyweds crawled into the back of the van and snuggled and kissed.

"The Shivering Sherlocks ladies are a hoot," Kellen said to Birdie.

They were. Tammy White seemed to be in charge; she herded them toward the seats, consulted her clipboard and told them their room numbers and who their roommates would be. When she was done, the other ladies saluted, laughed and teased her, then talked over each other in rapidly increasing volume. Debbie had no-nonsense iron gray hair, Candy had dyed hers a soft blond, but they were obviously twins. The ladies helped themselves to the hors d'oeuvres and pried into Kellen's and Birdie's backgrounds.

Nils Brooks came down the steps late, holding his computer case to his chest like a child he needed to protect. He ducked to get into the van, smacked his head, backed away and took off his rain-smeared glasses. He slipped them into his pocket.

Kellen caught a glimpse of his eyes. Brown, with thick black lashes.

Kellen took a long step back. She knew him. *Didn't she?*

"He's an *author*," Mrs. White told Birdie and Kellen, as if that explained everything.

Kellen watched from behind as he climbed into the seat in the back corner and scrunched away from the newlyweds. Those eyes… She remembered those eyes. But his face… No. She didn't remember him at all.

"He can write in my book anytime," Birdie quietly told Kellen.

Startled, Kellen raised her brows at Birdie.

"I'm a widow," Birdie said. "There's nothing wrong with my vision."

Kellen could hardly argue with that. He was nice to look at. And those eyes… "He's not what I expected. On the phone, he sounded impatient. The way he questioned me about the area—he thought he was the shitz. *That* man has a dimple."

"More than one, I'd imagine."

"I'm talking about the one in his chin." With everybody seated, Kellen got into the driver's seat.

Birdie lowered the jump seat, faced the guests and picked up the second box of hors d'oeuvres.

"Hey, folks!" The pilot stuck his head in the van, startling everyone. "It's getting dark. The weather's closing in. I've got ice on the wings and I'm not going to chance taking my plane out. Mind if I stay at the resort until it clears?"

CHAD GRIFFIN:
MALE, 40S, PILOT, ACCOMPLISHED WOMANIZER (IN HIS OWN MIND). EATS TOO MUCH, DRINKS TOO MUCH, DRAMATIZES HIS (UNLIKELY) MILITARY BACKGROUND. SHIFTLESS, LAZY, IRRITATING TO RESORT STAFF, BARNACLE-LIKE (DIFFICULT TO REMOVE).

Still, Kellen had no choice, so she said, "Of course, Chad, come on in."

He flung in his carry-on, slid into the passenger's

Teresa Zemaitis

grabbed a handful

The women reach for it, halted, her hand .
made the
a brief history of
the sea and sky and
activities.

right. with enthusiasm:
A voice this was free This looked like…
need the energy behind her.
jumped hard hands up.

something white
Feeling overreacted.
study this know?"
I saw some bodies

she pointed

Rain fell. inspired by damp palms on
and those eyes—
nervous.
thighs study the antiques

and smiled

wonder
"Why
"I spotted the

helped the ladies
my attention
her hand with picked up the
wiggled around, grinding in and
around here, there is no rain

grabbed a handful

reach for it,   halted, her hand

right.
right.   This looked like…
A   voice   behind her.

jumped hard

hands up.
Right.   overreacted.
Feeling
study this
I saw some bodies

Rain fell.   his glasses
those eyes—
her nervous   palms
thighs

wonder
"Why   asked.
"I spotted
your attention."

my attention   Covering
her hand   picked up
wiggled around, grinding
around here, there is no

ing other than a human woman that has that distinctive shape." He bent to look more closely.

She covered the bones with another napkin. "I'll show this to the Cape Charade policeman."

Nils Brooks stuck his hands into his pockets. "Let me know what he says." Turning away, he wandered back toward the portico and the lobby, and as he did, he called back, "But I'm right."

Oh! Too bad that he probably *was* right.

She sprinted across the soggy lawn toward the hotel wing where the remodelers were working, and as she ran, she called Temo. "Did you get that carcass picked up yet?"

"Not. Yet." She could hear the motor of his ATV, the wind blowing past the phone and his incredible frustration. "First I had to explain to two of the local idiots that, no, I'm not paying them to play games on their iPads. Then Smart Home called. They are neither."

"Smart, nor home? I am sorry, Temo. Let me know what you find as soon as you find the, um, skeleton." She hung up on him, then called Sheri Jean Hagerty. "I have an emergency. Can I postpone for an hour?"

"You had an emergency yesterday."

"Did you hear about the carcass found on the grounds this morning?"

"What about it?"

"One of the coyotes dragged off a chunk and a guest saw it." Which was true. Nils Brooks had seen it.

No one understood the megrims of some guests as well as the guest experience manager. "Let me know as soon as you're free."

"Will do." Kellen ducked under the tape warning guests not to enter, opened the door and walked to-

~~ward the still-unfinished concierge lounge.~~ Sheets of ~~plastic hung over the door; she pushed them aside and~~ ~~entered a hell of leaning ladders, a roaring belt sander~~ ~~and swirling wood dust.~~ AND

~~Lloyd Magnuson stood alone in the middle of the~~ ~~room, wearing ear protection and a filtering mask, and~~ ~~foaming at the cornice board. He was sanding.~~

~~Kellen waited until he paused, then shouted, "Lloyd."~~

~~LLOYD MAGNUSON:~~
~~MALE. 5'7". 180 LBS. BALDING IN FRONT, DREAD-~~
~~LOCKS IN BACK. AGE 40. LOOKS 30. MADE CHA-~~
~~RADE POLICEMAN. DUTIES INCLUDE DEALING~~
~~WITH: SPEEDING TICKETS, VEHICLE COLLISIONS,~~
~~UNRULY TOURISTS. MAIN INCOME FROM CAR-~~
~~PENTRY WORK. CREATING OBJETS D'ART FROM~~
~~DRIFTWOOD, NETS, FISHING NETS, FLOATS.~~
~~SELLS THEM TO CHARADE GROCERS.~~

~~He looked up, startled, dropped his ear protection~~ ~~around his neck, wiped his sleeve over his safety glasses~~ ~~and pulled his mask to the top of his head. "Now what?"~~

~~They'd had an argument about the size of the cor-~~ ~~nice board. Annie had taken Kellen's side and he was~~ still irritated. of a

~~"I need you to be a policeman,"~~ ~~she pulled off the top~~ ~~napkin and held the bones cradled in the other napkin.~~ ~~"I~~ found this in the rhododendrons ~~and I was wondering~~ ~~that is, I thought it looked like...~~

~~Lloyd pulled a pouch out of his pocket, unzipped~~ ~~it and pulled out a clean rag. He wiped off his safety~~ ~~glasses. "Yep, I'm a hunter, and~~ ~~a hip ~~ He studied it ~~"The animal I've ever seen."~~

a human shape a body.

beneath her leather shoes.

the remains.

They looked questioningly.

"How do you want this photographed?" She didn't From a distance and close in. "Do you know the last time

Neither do I.

How do you know

She didn't want to know. But for the first time, she looked. the smaller bones One hip bone remained leg bones The rib cage the spine Wisps of hair the skull…

"Or maybe hated all women," Temo said. "There's a lot of that in this world." Winter is not finished

Kellen had to say it. "High tide. Really high tide. She could be from one of the sea caves." a silent promi

"Sure. Wow. Murder. Definitely need to show this to Sheriff Kwinault. If she—" he gestured at the body "—washed out of the sea caves, maybe the murder took place here." t's never too late for love!

"God forbid," Kellen said fervently. Keep Your

"Could mean there's a murderer on the loose." With a towel, Lloyd picked up a grubby piece of rubbery material and a torn piece of faded cloth and offered them to Kellen. "Take this and show it to the women at the resort. Ask them if they recognize the shoe or the material and remember who they belong to. Maybe we can figure something out that way." Call 811 Before You D

Kellen looked at the misshapen thing. A shoe. The sole of a tennis shoe. And a swatch of material.

She didn't take it. "I'm not showing this to the staff!

Life must be lived and curiosity kept aliv

"It you don't show it to them and somebody else gets murdered, you're responsible," Lloyd said.

She didn't need more guilt to deal with. Yet— "This body has been around for a while and no one else has been killed." Three trains one underground

Temo stuck his two cents in. "That we know of."

She looked down at her friend. She thought of all the staff who were on vacation, how some of them had already called to say they weren't coming back. She thought of all the guests who came and went, and never returned. Temo had a point. Still, she argued, "No one's going to know who wore this tennis shoe. It's just...a tennis shoe. I can't even tell what color it is. Or was."

Go for the Hot Chocolate.

t would be useless if the world were perfect.

"You have a better idea for identifying the body?"

real-estate values bounce back

"A coroner?" she suggested. Each of us is a seed

"We haven't got a coroner. We've got an undertaker. He's not busy and he likes it that way. But…good idea." Lloyd pulled out his cell phone. "The county coroner is in Virtue Falls, too. Mike Sun has dealt with this kind of thing before—murder and whatnot. I'll drive the bones up, deliver them to Mike, talk to Sheriff Kwinault and see if either one of them can figure out something about the death and who it is." avoid economic calamity

"It's a nasty drive in this weather," Kellen said.

"I don't mind." Lloyd sounded positively cheerful. "I've got friends in Virtue Falls. Good time for a visit!"

"Go on, Kellen," Temo said. "I'll get the photos taken. I'll get her up off the ground. You're not doing any good here." and it is always spring

Kellen knew she shouldn't make Temo do something she wouldn't do herself. But it wasn't so much *wouldn't* as *couldn't*, at least she couldn't without vomiting. "Thank you Smell Gas. Act Fast. Gingerly, she took the towel by the four corners, carried it back to the ATV and drove back as fast as she'd driven out. She didn't want to go in the front lobby and face the guests, so she parked by the back door to the spa, the one Destiny Longacre had left open for her boyfriend. Before she got close, Mara swung the heavy metal door open.

The wind caught it and slammed it against the wall.

Both women grabbed it, fought with it, got it under control A seismic change is underway

"What a wretched day." Kellen meant more than just the weather. Help a New Yorker in Need

"I heard." Mara had that significant tone in her voice.

I'm enjoying the empty nest possibilities.

Kellen turned to her. "How did you hear?"

"Lloyd Magnuson called Sheri Jean and asked for a storage box. Said he had to drive something out to Mike Sun in Virtue Falls. She knew you were picking up something the scavengers brought in. She figured it out. A natural death?"

Kellen shook her head.

"Damn it." Mara looked around at her determined powerful domain. "Damn it," she said again. "Do you know who the body is?"

Kellen held up the towel she had twisted shut. "That's what we're supposed to deduce using a piece of cloth and part of a shoe."

"This way. Don't drop it, and don't make a fuss." She led Kellen to the spa waiting room, where nine anxious employees waited.

Sheri Jean + three concierge staff.

FRANCES:
34, CONCIERGE/FRONT DESK, CHICAGO NATIVE, TOUGH, SARCASTIC. EMPLOYED 7 YRS.

GERALD:
MALE, 42, FRONT DESK, GUATEMALAN, FLUENT IN SPANISH. EMPLOYED YEARS.

TRENT:
37, DESK STAFF, CAPE CHARADE NATIVE. EMPLOYED 7 YRS., THEN SERVED PRISON TERM FOR BREAKING AND ENTERING. REEMPLOYED 4 YRS.

Mara + four spa staff.

How many "scraps"

in a

voice

There's one I've heard, but

don't want to think of

That cloth against skin dragged

over to

study the scrap It was at one time

lightweight natural and worn

in the summer but

exposure to rain will do that a

lot of

talking like

I understand how color

fades and

you

captured a snapshot

to review it but

Maybe

that doesn't get us

anywhere.

Even more impatient are we

to a body based on a scrap of cloth

10

v1

a profound silence,

soothing harp music

Title one smooth movement

"It's a ring."

her voice trembled.

v2 Destiny nodded her head up and down, up and down.

glasses full.

offering fine wine.

a Celtic knot with a purple topaz.

Destiny covered her face

"Kellen said it was" wasn't a natural death, and I have to say I agree.

Kellen sipped a wonderful dampness in a mouth that had been dry for too long.

forced her to drive,

," Destiny

nces taunted.

and yet, how could she ~~have~~ survive

somewhere else? Des-
tiny

spoke the way
she

agreed

, groping for a way to
make this come out right.

death was
grieved, we a family.

his serene voice he
watches out and we trust

arms clasped

encouragingly

"I

understand

you can stay."
my red eyes
lit up

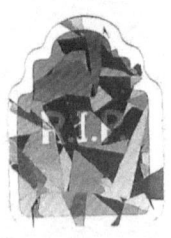

question

the

kind nightmare

trust and

logic abandoned

to memories

turned to

ice.

'What

turned and looked

to me

alone waiting

w a s

a grinned Gruesome death

today

her

hands

know

This is different.

the

storm

hurried

in the air.

"No. That is, Mr. Gilfilen says to let him alone, and he got that word from Mrs. DiLuca."

So Annie knew. "What is it we're ignoring?"

Axel pulled his belt up over his belly. "He breaks into storage rooms and sometimes he takes stuff."

"Like shower caps and shoe shine kits?" She was incredulous again.

"Can't ever have too many shower caps." Axel laughed again.

She did not like this man. Her gaze slid to the old-fashioned big black bank vault, the one they used to store the guests' valuables and the resort's records. Mr. Gilfilen had assured her the locking mechanism was new, only selected staff could access it and he had made her one of the privileged few. She hoped that was true, she would hesitate to trust Axel with anyone's cash or jewels. "Who do we have on the floor?"

"McGladrey." Axel brought one monitor into sharp focus on a man in a dark suit standing in the gift shop staring at a display of candy bars. "He's a good guy, one of our best security men. He's as faithful as an old dog."

As they watched, McGladrey slid a Twix into his jacket and made a run for it.

"Faithful, but not honest," she said.

Axel broke a sweat.

She studied the monitors, watched a smiling Sheri Jean mingle with the guests, saw the miles of empty corridors and the outdoor entrances.

"This guy's interesting." Axel pointed at Nils Brooks "He came in from his cottage, looked around the lobby, then wandered the halls taking notes."

"He's a writer." She felt as if she was making excuses for him. "But even for a writer, that's odd behavior."

rime laid on her doorstep was—everybody looked like
villain. "Mr. Gilfilen set everything up before he left,
o he told me. I'll occasionally drop by, but call me if
o... anything suspicious."

"R ght." Axel pulled a tissue out of a box and blot-
ed his face, then blew his nose. With sweaty sincerity,
e said, "I'll watch, Miss Adams. We don't want any-
ling like murder happening again."

At least he understood that.

She made it to Annie's office without interruption—
hat was one advantage to being at an almost empty
esort—up two flights of stairs to a wide set of dou-
le doors. A square glass-covered table with a well-
onstructed model of the resort and its grounds dom-
lated the center of the spacious room. Annie's desk
aced the door. Kellen's desk faced the window. A
mall, comfortable seating area with a gas fireplace
nd bookshelves hugged one corner. A dusty CB radio,
ept for emergencies, hid in a cabinet with paper clips
nd typewriter ribbons.

Kellen used the house phone to make the call.

Leo picked up. "What is it?" His voice sounded tired
nd rough.

"Mr. Di Luca, we have a crisis here at the resort."

"Do your best to handle it."

Not the response she expected. "You don't under-
tand. We found a body. A dead body. A corpse."

"You don't understand. Annie moved here and col-
apsed. She's got pneumonia. She's in the hospital on
xygen and she's in the middle of an arthritic flare-up
he's suffering, maybe dying."

Pity and grief caught her around the throat.
nce. Www www. What can I do for you? For A

She wouldn't ~~accept it, and~~ she wouldn't ~~~~

~~casually drop~~ information like ~~pieces of bread.~~

All of us ~~are~~ running ~~away~~ from something.

"Doubt ~~made~~ the landscape. ~~nothing~~ happened ~~another body~~ shrugged. ~~overworked~~

~~the sleeve of~~ clean ~~glass~~ between Cape Charade ~~and safe.~~

~~death.~~ and nothing's happened since. ~~overreacting~~

"Yes. Possibly. But ~~a killer~~ threatened ~~her,~~ frightened ~~her,~~ managed to capture ~~and hold her long enough~~

12

the number one slot,

                      leading

  The newlyweds
    Shivering
dressed in costumes: tie and fe-
dora;
fringe and feathers;   red

        painted high-arched eyebrows

      rocked as a stout

    self
urked in hotel hallways,
       enjoying

      shared experience

he pushed

She sounded manic

I'm trying

I

will survive

without you

he didn't know

fault

He

was

angst-ridden

totally heartless.

For the first time,

Show me a man who can

she

was right.

R Hope 9.23

death and

an orca sighting...

he
poured himself a hefty glass of wine.

Look at him
Those ladies don't want *him*

trying to engage   in conversation.

"She's leaning away."

couldn't
have made her disdain more obvious.

"Have you met him?"

Johns," Frances said, the ghost of a grin. "I'll tell
Mrs. _____ to check the governor when he's in."

"How often does the power _____?"

"Not too often, but when it does, it's nice if the gen-
erator is functional. Look out, here comes _____
and she looks like she's on the warpath."

Kellen swiveled on the balls of her feet. "Shari Jean,
I've got you down for a murder night."

"We've got no _____ in our casino," Shari Jean's
voice rose.

Kellen something but a wind of a storm and a long,
dark and whatever in ___. The reading from door whirled
suddenly. A gust of wind swept the lobby; it knocked
petals off the flower arrangements and sent papers fly-
ing.

Kellen and Shari Jean stood _____

_____ "Door closed," swooped his hand
in. "Sorry." Jean _____ something about death longer,
Blaine Laurent."

"Priscilla," Shari Jean whispered, "She's sending
us a message."

Startled, Kellen studied her white face. Shari Jean
really believed, and this picture so unlike her. "What
message would that be?"

Somehow a breeze broke the big window facing
the sea.

Frances puffed and laughed.

Shari _____ "Priscilla is not going to rest
until her killer is brought to justice."

13

*The
leaf*

on the
bed

was
only
getting
more
lonely. So lonely. When
thrashing
and blowing   about, she felt
the edge of   love
without companionship. But

someone remembered her, even if   only an

old friend

laughed and laughed. "He was right." She pointed at the photo. "He was right."

"Who was right, Mother?" Erin had been a pretty girl, always tall for her age and big-boned, but with startling hazel eyes, thick blond hair and a wide mouth. Yet no man had ever been interested in her. Or perhaps she'd never been interested in any man other than Gregory, not since that moment when Waddington Lykke brought Sylvia and Gregory home from the hospital, put the squalling infant into Erin's eager arms and said, "This is your younger brother. You must take care of him. He's the Lykke family heir, and very precious."

Now Erin carried an extra twenty pounds, but she was still attractive. She ran Lykke Industries with an iron hand...and Sylvia feared her daughter.

"Mother!" Erin took both Sylvia's shoulders and shook her hard. "Why are you laughing?"

Sylvia's neck snapped, and she sobered. "You're such a bully."

"What?" Erin rocked with annoyance. "What was so funny?"

"That." Sylvia pointed at the screen. "He was right. He didn't kill her. There she is, Cecilia, alive and well. The dear child does look well."

Erin shoved her mother out of the computer chair and sat and stared. In a faraway voice, she said, "I've found her. Gregory, I've found her."

"There's nothing wrong with her being alive. Gregory's rotting in his grave."

Erin looked at her in fury. "He is not!"

"So's Waddington. Nobody ever deserved death as much as your father. He was a cruel man. When I married him, I thought I'd married a prince. But he hurt me.

All the time, he hurt me." Sylvia wandered toward the bed. She had forgotten Erin was here, forgotten why she was on her feet. She was lost in the past, in memories that brought tears to her cheeks. "He never gave me anything except two children who were monsters like him. I knew there was something wrong with Erin. When I found my kitten with its neck broken, I cried. I thought Waddington had done it. But Erin said I loved the kitten more than her, so she killed it. Until then I didn't know about Erin. But Gregory... I knew from the first moment I looked into his eyes that he was warped, like a looking glass all distorted. When he married that poor girl, I thought... I'm still ashamed, you know? That I didn't stand up for her. But Waddington hurt me so much I didn't have any courage left. He said I was nothing and he made me nothing. I'm nothing."

Erin touched Sylvia's arm.

Sylvia turned and looked at her in surprise. "Dear, what are you doing here? How wonderful to see you. I grow so lonely here..."

"Do you know who this is?" Erin pointed at a picture on the computer monitor.

"Oh! Oh! It is Cecilia! Gregory was right. She lived. How good to know she lived." Sylvia laughed and thought how good it was to laugh.

Erin lifted her hand.

Abruptly sober, Sylvia cowered.

Erin dropped her head, took an impatient breath and said, "Gregory wanted her dead. Don't you remember?"

"I remember."

"When we brought him back to the house, Gregory told me to finish the job that he failed to do. That was what Gregory wanted. Don't you understand?"

When I'm here alone at night,

to breathe

security

is

safe,

small

jagged

weapon

you

trained

I didn't expect to find myself with

you

Remember v

the

mess.

only.

You

appreciate

innocent

people

I

could

darken

them

clean up after the storm

promise.

wonder

not as bad

not as bad

Think

be happy

tired.

look up.

sleep

look up spiral

feel safe

ghosts

grief

remember

remember   remember

the sun rise

R███████████████████████████████king-
ing ███ and returning it, ████ because of Kellen's
sleepless night.

"You were a legend. ████ said ████████████e
k████"

"A████████████████████████████████
a███████████ told her of her discharge, as if he knew
████████████████ as if he ████████████████
████████████ he could do███████d who would die.

N██████████████████████████████████
g██████████ old maintenance████████████
████████████████████████████ for 1957 Dual
████████"

"Wh███" K████ felt the awe. "I ████████████e
████t."

"I██████████████████████████ most of the
f████████████████, recycle it, I'm another ou████
f████████████████

K████████████████ TH██"S███████?"

██ot tonight. I'm ████████████████ you should be
████

██████████t for a few minutes, I n███████ething to
do████████ hands. It takes ██████████ off ... what's ██
r██████d."

"████████████ then. You have ████████████████
that████████████████████████████ and I hav███t
b████████████

K████████████████████ug of hot chocolate, p████d
██ a pan of Birdie's ████████████ UD████ onto
her forehead████████████████████████ponies and
██████

██████████████ tone, Birdie said "I told the g███

something didn't add up.

Kellen

watching

needed to

run

and try turn and wave his

hands He'd lost his key

She wanted to

sleep in peace, quiet and comfort between cool, clean sheets. she crawled

toward

the west, toward the ocean and the place where

the rain started. Cecilia

watched

the storm coming in the

ocean would erase evidence,

She didn't know how to turn on the

controls

Stuff happened.

fast,

driving

blind on a twisty two-lane highway scared,

15

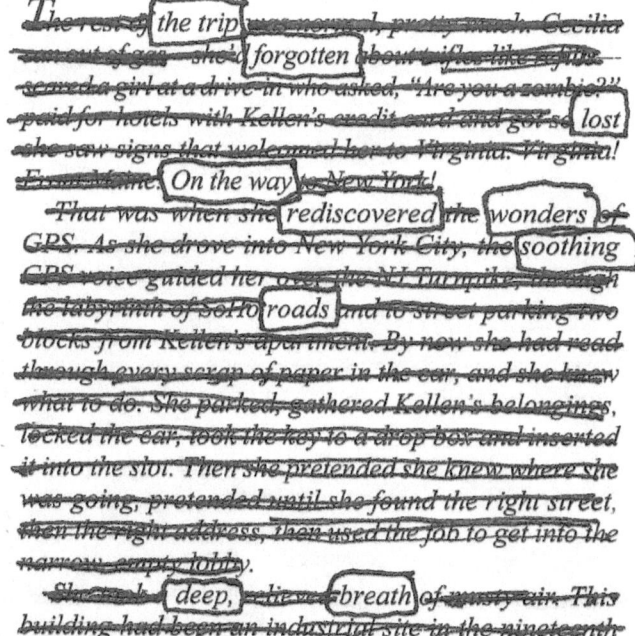

The rest of ~~the trip~~ *the trip* ~~was normal, pretty much. Cecilia ran out of gas~~ she'd *forgotten* ~~about it, like, like~~ *lost* ~~seemed a girl at a drive-in who asked, "Are you a zombie?" paid for hotels with Kellen's credit card and got so~~ *lost* ~~she saw signs that welcomed her to Virginia. Virginia! From Maine.~~ *On the way* ~~to New York!~~

~~That was when she~~ *rediscovered* ~~the~~ *wonders* ~~of GPS. As she drove into New York City, the~~ *soothing* ~~GPS voice guided her over the NJ Turnpike, through the labyrinth of SoHo~~ *roads* ~~and to street parking two blocks from Kellen's apartment. By now she had read through every scrap of paper in the car, and she knew what to do. She parked, gathered Kellen's belongings, locked the car, took the key to a drop box and inserted it into the slot. Then she~~ pretended she knew where she was going, ~~pretended until she found the right street, then the right address, then used the fob to get into the narrow, empty lobby.~~

~~She took a~~ *deep* ~~lit in a~~ *breath* ~~of musty air. This building had been an industrial site in the nineteenth~~

~~*sank back onto the couch, pulled the throw over her head and wallowed in guilt and darkness.*~~

The darkness was growing...

~~Kellen woke.~~

~~She was still in her clothes in the chair beside the bed,~~ tense, sweaty, ~~cold and cramped beneath the patterned throw.~~

~~The darkness was *not* growing. In fact, the room's automatic night-light provided enough illumination to see the outlines of the furniture and walls. She pulled~~ her phone out of her pocket, ~~checked for internet, and when she saw it pop up, she sighed in relief.~~ She stretched her stiff muscles. ~~In the daytime, the window looked away from the resort and the cottages and toward the dock and the Pacific Ocean. Now,~~ on this rainy, moonless night, ~~she saw nothing.~~ Nothing.

Then ~~one single bright light shone in the dark. A flashlight?~~ A lantern?

It blinked off.

~~She blinked, too. Was that the remnant of~~ a nightmare?

~~No, someone was out there. Lost? Alone?~~ *Looking for the body* ~~they had lost? She flipped off the night-light and moved through utter darkness toward the window.~~

~~The light outside came on again and swung in a circle on the ground, then up in the air.~~

~~Kellen stepped back to avoid being spotted.~~

~~Ridiculous, but automatic.~~

~~She glanced at the time.~~ Two forty-five a.m. ~~Whoever it was either wasn't afraid of being seen or wanted~~

~~to be seen. Or their meeting hadn't~~ occurred ~~as they expected and they were desperate. Or…or she didn't know.~~

~~She did know~~ the night was pitch-dark, rain rattled against the window ~~like sleet and today they'd found a decomposing body out on the flats. Had someone found~~ another one?

~~The~~ light flashed ~~around~~ again.

~~Damn it. Annie left and less than twenty-four hours later, Kellen was up to her ass in alligators and it was hard to remember that her directive was to drain the swamp. She watched that light, willing it to go out permanently, and when that didn't happen, she cursed as only an Army officer could curse, got her~~ Glock ~~and~~ strapped ~~it~~ into her shoulder holster, ~~pulled her rain gear on over her clothes and headed out.~~

~~As soon as she stepped foot on the porch, the wind caught her breath and whipped it away. Sleet blew beneath the overhang and~~ stung her face. ~~This was going to be one fast trip out to check on…whatever. Maybe she should pretend she hadn't seen anything.~~ ~~But no.~~ ~~She owed it to Annie to find out if they'd been dealt another tragedy. Holding the handrail, she groped her way down the stairs. She took small steps toward her ATV.~~

A man's voice ~~behind her said,~~ "Don't ~~do this.~~"

~~Not a moment of hesitation.~~ She whipped ~~around in the turning kick Mara had been teaching her. She should have struck his throat. But she~~ slipped ~~and~~ landed ~~a strike on his hip. She~~ kicked ~~again, aiming high.~~

He blocked.

She landed ~~a solid strike against his arm.~~

~~She~~ attacked.

He parried.

~~She landed good hits, but somehow~~ she never did

" She

was noth-
ing more than a ▪▪▪ darkness, ▪▪▪
trying to ▪▪▪ play ▪▪▪

When she stepped
out of her ▪▪▪

▪▪▪ cynicism ▪▪▪ she hadn't lost herself
▪▪▪. So she would listen, ▪▪▪ wait
▪▪▪ mysterious ▪▪▪
on an empty plain where ▪▪▪ a body had been ▪▪▪.
She followed ▪▪▪ light ▪▪▪
▪▪▪ ran up the steps, unlocked ▪▪▪
▪▪▪ time—opened it ▪▪▪
▪▪▪ an inviting ▪▪▪ of bright-
ness ▪▪▪.
She glanced toward the ▪▪▪.
▪▪▪ light ▪▪▪
She slowly followed, ▪▪▪
▪▪▪.

▪▪▪, moved into
the ▪▪▪ water and put ▪▪▪
▪▪▪ her, ▪▪▪
▪▪▪ arms and ▪▪▪ ankles.
▪▪▪ in the open ▪▪▪.
▪▪▪ aimless ▪▪▪ vanished. ▪▪▪
▪▪▪ smart enough to wear rain ▪▪▪

There's a lot of
looted treasure. Enough   for

two mugs   their
     Hot   herbal.
          kind

     latch   the door

                              place
the end table
     and   chair facing

          the kitchen.

               I'll

          use   hot water and
two cups of
               ginger

There.   you   relax
enough   to
     smile, those dimples
          need to
          revive

piece of art, literature and relic. The previously ran-
dom looting became organized. The locals were either
pushed out or conscripted and forced to find valuable
artifacts and hand them over to the terrorists.

Google showed no answer to her question, nothing
but the usual hodgepodge of internet weirdness. "You,
um, don't seem to be a member of the MFAA."

"I didn't choose to post my unfortunate promotion.
That would be stupid, wouldn't it?"

It would. But she didn't have to admit it out loud.

"Search for the Brooks family of Charleston, South
Carolina," he said. "It'll come up."

She did as he suggested and found an old and formi-
dable dynasty—and there he was, part of a family sho
that included an elderly marriarch, a nervous-looking
mother, six languid uncles, no father and enough cous-
ins to populate a small island. Which apparently they
did and had for generations among varying amounts
of scandal.

Kellen flicked a glance at Nils's photo and then a
his face.

NILS BROOKS:

MALE, 30S, 6' 180 LBS. BROWN HAIR (BLOND
ROOTS?), BROWN EYES (COMPELLING), LONG
LASHES, MILITARY HAIRCUT, NARROW JAW, DARK-
RIMMED GLASSES (USED AS DISGUISE), CUTE,
HANDSOME, NERDY, CONFIDENT, CLOTHING,
EXPENSIVE, WELL-WORN, MEMBER OF SOUTH
CAROLINA'S DISTINGUISHED BROOKS DYNASTY,
GRADUATE OF DUKE UNIVERSITY, LEADER OF
NEWLY RE-FORMED MFAA (AS REPORTED BY HIM).

Perhaps her background made her too suspicious.

Maybe she was smart to be suspicious. Her first impression of Nils Brooks had proved to be massively inaccurate. He had set out to deceive, and he had succeeded. In so many ways, he reminded her of Gregory.

"You're saying the terrorists don't care how they achieve their goals or who or what is hurt in the process?"

"Terrorists are terrorists. They want the world to go up in flames, and they don't care how it comes about."

"As long as their cause is the winner."

"Of course."

"What you're telling me is interesting. Fishy, but interesting. But the job of the MFAA in World War II was to—" she looked at her screen and read "'— to safeguard historic and cultural monuments from war damage, and, as the conflict came to a close, to find and return works of art and other items of cultural importance that had been stolen by the Nazis or hidden for safekeeping.' I can't believe the MFAA in its current inception will be terrorist fighters."

"Reopening the MFAA was our idea. Jessica's and mine. The declared intention of the agency is to interrupt the flow of cash. That's the only reason we were able to convince the Feds to green-light the restoration of the agency."

Good, succinct, sensible answer. She wanted good, succinct, sensible answers, because everything she'd looked up so far checked out. But was it possible to manipulate the internet to make everything conveniently fit? Of course it was. Lies were made truth all the time. The MFAA website was a dot-gov website, so maybe that made it supervised?

Yes, by someone in the US government.

He retrieved a long piece of paper from the stack on the kitchen counter and held it toward her. "Here's a list of antiquities shipments that we've identified over the past five years and, if possible, what they were and where they were delivered."

She stood up, grabbed the spreadsheet, returned to her seat and studied it. "On the East Coast, it looks as if most art and artifacts were European or Middle Eastern in origin and delivered to wealthy collectors across the country. West Coast—Far Eastern and Central and South American artifacts. Makes sense."

He pulled out another spreadsheet, handed it to her. "Here's a list of the bodies we've found and approximate dates of their deaths." He sat back down. "We assume others are undiscovered."

She examined the list. Eight bodies over the past five years, on both coasts, in remote coastal areas off the beaten track. She compared the two lists. "Huh. The center of the action seems to be here."

He leaned back in his seat and radiated satisfaction. "That's what Jessie saw, too. What I saw."

"With shipments coming in on both coasts—"

"Which we at first didn't recognize."

"—and a murder here and a murder there..."

"We couldn't see a pattern for a long time."

"It's not certain."

"It is if we all saw it. That's why I decided to bring you in. I've read your profile. You can put it all together."

Yes, she could. "Who's in charge of the smuggling?" she asked.

CHRIST

in a weird way

knows

He

is

looked at it in horror

Too much
conniption

to keep up with

'he wants

the

Challenge

to

fight

himself

he wants to be on TV

all

The

publicity

!

messiah

"I don't know ~~if that makes~~ her ~~more of a suspect
or less.~~"

"~~I don't know, either." She stopped. Turned to~~ face
~~him. I have~~ a question ~~for you. I'm smart enough. What~~
if it's ~~me?~~"

"~~It seemed~~ hard to run ~~a smuggling ring~~ from ~~a~~ war
~~zone with the Army directing your~~ every move ~~and a
certain general and his aide keeping you~~ under observa-
tion ~~with the intention of using you for code~~ breaking."

"~~He'd heard about that, had he? Nils Brooks knew too
much, and she didn't know enough. So she went fish-
ing.~~ "~~I have another question. If you're~~ trying to crack ~~a
smuggling ring, what are you doing in here? Shouldn't
you be~~ out ~~in~~ the ~~dark and the~~ storm ~~spying on the
smugglers,~~ seeing ~~who they are,~~ what ~~they're doing?"~~

"~~I didn't come to disable the smuggling. It's not as
simple as that."~~

"~~That~~ would ~~interrupt~~ the flow ~~of cash."~~

"~~Only temporarily, and only at this site. No. My ul-
timate goal is, and I bet, to identify and~~ capture the ~~Li-
brarian. He~~ or she ~~isn't going to be the one out there
collecting the goods or doing a drop-off. That's what
flunkies are for." He reached into his pocket, pulled
out his~~ black ~~rimmed glasses and slipped them~~ on ~~with
the seeming~~ confidence of Superman ~~disappearing~~ be-
hind ~~Clark~~ Kent's disguise. "~~I'm the author with writer's
block who wanders~~ the ~~resort looking~~ for inspiration
~~in all the wrong places and observing everyone with a
profiler's eye."~~

"~~Okay.~~"

"~~Okay?" She'd managed to surprise him.~~

"~~That's what I figured. I wanted to hear~~ you say ~~it.
I have to go. At this moment~~; I'm ~~way more~~ afraid ~~of~~

More than I am of the Librarian. Later!" Kellen jumped off his porch.

He called, "Think about suspects!"

She lifted her hand. Rain splattered her in the face. Somewhere behind the roiling storm clouds, dawn was breaking. She started down the path to her cottage, thinking, *Race to the resort, shower and change, call and check on Annie. And Leo. But mostly Annie.* Then—

"Kellen!" Mara stood under the light on Kellen's porch, clothed in her close-fitting, water-shedding running gear. "What were you doing out at this hour?"

"Nils Brooks got lost on the way to his cottage." Which was the truth.

"He doesn't seem to be very bright."

"Agreed." Anybody who arrived alone to seek out a murderous smuggler didn't get a gold star for smarts, at least not on Kellen's chart.

"Do you like him?" Mara sounded anxious.

"No." Not him, nor his astute observations and his blunt way of attacking. "Hang on. Let me duck inside and we'll get going." Inside, she shed her clothes and stashed her pistol. She pulled on her running gear, then hurried out to meet Mara. She said, "I can't do kickboxing this morning. Too much to do, not enough sleep. Maybe tomorrow. Let's run!" She leaped off her own porch and headed along the lighted pathways, headed toward the behemoth of a hotel where her day would begin.

After a minute, Mara was running at her heels, shouting, "How do you expect me to win the International Ninja Challenge if you're not dedicated to my cause?"

"Determination!" Kellen shouted back. "Yours!" Today, she didn't allow Mara to set the pace. Not today. Today, Kellen was in charge.

— Tryn

battling and banging their heads

he would be on his way,

she ceased trying

Could he be more inconsiderate?

ression in place, interviewing the various recruiters the staff for his book."

found Sheri Jean in the lobby speaking with two of the ... on from San Francisco

her **daughter.**

Sheri Jean ... ed teeth sort of way and introduced ... is is Mrs. Kazin and her daughter, Jasmine. Th ... two ladies would like to ck out two days earl ... ined we have a policy of, in these ... deposit, but they ho ...

expressed unhappiness

I thought ... pe of policy.

smil ... at the ... en-year ... Jasmine. "Th
we ... **ghastly,** asn't it."

dark just el ... **night**
for ... The ...
is it always ... ed.

... my first ... e mey ... ed me ... inter
stor ... have been ... sually ferocious." K ... put his hand on Sheri Jean ... oulder and ... heri Jean ... inch of rejection. ... of course we'll refun ... e deposit.

... d like ... ou in the ... ubby, where Frances wa ... es, a bowl of apples ... she sounded ... to ... **like the adolescent she was.**

Then you'd be ... move on with your ... Kazin watch ... aughter leave, their ... ... We ... for ... he ...

she had nightmares. ... ivorce ...

* * *

the world

caught

the corners of that

ghost,

an old memory that

withered

and...

needed

care

she couldn't

She had to
She prepared

she descended

snapping *spill-*
ing,

in the future

please stop

crying

without drawing breath

the ~~each pocket~~ birth ~~hung~~ around her neck. no longer safe

19

awake,

her child,

her best

child, the young

Ellen didn't remember anything else. She dug the heels of her palms into her eyes. She did not remember anything else.

What had she forgotten?

hadn't gone from her life. What had she done?

The phone
then leaned to answer.

his

"Rae will understand." Max lifted his hand to stop any further objections. "We already had our private Christmas on December twenty-fifth, and when she's here in the midst of the family, I hardly see her. I'll explain it to her, and you know her—she has a generous spirit. She *will* understand."

Leo stood and faced off with Max. "*You* don't understand. It's not that easy."

"Of course it is." Max was used to being right, and to getting his way. "I'll leave today."

"First come and see Annie. She has things to say to you about the new assistant manager."

"So there *is* something wrong with her."

"Max! Stop jumping to conclusions! It's not her. It's *you*."

Max took a step back. Leo was always loud—he was slightly deaf—but never so emphatic. "Leo, what's wrong?"

Leo opened the door to Annie's room.

Annie's happy voice floated out, "Max, dear! So good to see you!"

Leo stepped in. "Max wants to go to handle security at the resort."

"That's a good idea! Except…" Annie's voice lost its euphoria. "Oh, dear."

Max could not imagine what was wrong with Leo and Annie. Of course, he didn't have much of an imagination. "I don't understand."

"There's no way you could." Leo gestured him in. "Go, sit down with Annie and listen."

in costume,

just poisoned.

"Oh. While

you're dead, would you care for

frozen grapes, smoked

with yogurt fruit dip

It's red." And a little

gruesome,

"I'll have one of each."

feed me

fork wrapped in

copper-she knew she would

never leave

opened wide.

half-eaten

already

glass

and

Yearning

not your concern,

care of themselves and others. Finally, she asked them to report to her anything they observed that struck them as peculiar, and thanked them for their continued diligence. She pressed Send, shut down the computer and the lights and sat in the dark room.

She had found herself unable to tell Mr. Gilfilen about Nils. She considered Mr. Gilfilen a trustworthy man, but she wasn't willing to jeopardize a federal sting operation based on her belief.

She knew she would not tell Nils about Mr. Gilfilen. She didn't completely trust Nils.

She didn't trust Sheri Jean. Or Mara. Most definitely not Chad Griffin. Adrian and Mitch she believed would guard her back in a combat situation, but when it came to making a profit by whatever means? She felt a wobble in her trust-o-meter.

She couldn't even confide in Birdie or Temo. Anything she said would put them in danger. So she would say nothing. She would tell no one what she knew from any source; she remembered her aunt's favorite saying, "Of course I can keep secrets, it's the people I tell them to who can't keep them."

This news about Lloyd Magnuson changed everything. He'd gone to the Virtue Falls coroner with the body of one of the Librarian's victims...and disappeared. Sure, it was possible he'd hit the bars and run into trouble. But no one had seen him, and seriously, who went on a bender with a plastic container of rotting flesh in the trunk?

So what exactly had happened? The Librarian had disposed of Priscilla's body somewhere close to the resort on the coast, it had washed ashore, and when the identity of the body became known, the Librarian had been alarmed. Perhaps having the body examined by a coroner might somehow lead to the Librarian's identity.

Yes. What they'd discovered had worried the Librarian and made him, or her, take extraordinary measures to reacquire Priscilla's body, and what happened to Lloyd Magnuson as a result didn't matter. Except it did. The guy's only crime was being a part-time policeman.

Kellen had, she realized, cratered in on herself, erecting that familiar ice wall between herself and everyone else, the way she had after the explosion, in those traumatic days in New York and on the grim streets of Philadelphia…

Turning on the desk light, she pulled a yellow tablet close, got a pen and in her brain pulled up the files for each person she deemed a suspect. If she believed everything Nils Brooks had told her, and she more or less did, then the Librarian was one of these people. Probably. And if she or he had a couple of flunkies, they'd be on the list, too. Probably.

She jotted down each detail about each person.

Then she checked vacations. She knew when Jessica had been killed, so she looked for the employees who had been gone in January. Which was just about everybody except her, who wanted to hunker down here, and Birdie, who didn't want to go home to Detroit. Oh, and Carson Lennex had been in Machu Picchu, a fact that hadn't mattered before and now seemed grossly ominous. She weeded out a few names, but—the Librarian ran a big operation at multiple sites. What size was the Librarian's organization?

Oh. And a large number of the Yearning Sands staff

—jo reyes-boitel

DEAD

still   wrong and

was   here

So many   and none   easily

red.

tore   paper and   into   over-
size coat,   headed down   dining.
late;   something to eat.

here   found   digging through the freezer
and loading   dinners into

insulated   bag.

How   Did you
find

the point   being cut.

clear

Everything   didn't look

fine.   tired,   two days

of dark   scowl

down over his eyes.

More problems in

and

back into the depths of the freezer

another   look

into the bag.   my

prison   other than that

something   isn't it

First time   prison,   a

bitter set   mouth.   more

than once.

now   shut   a little too hard.

placed   with

You

edged away.

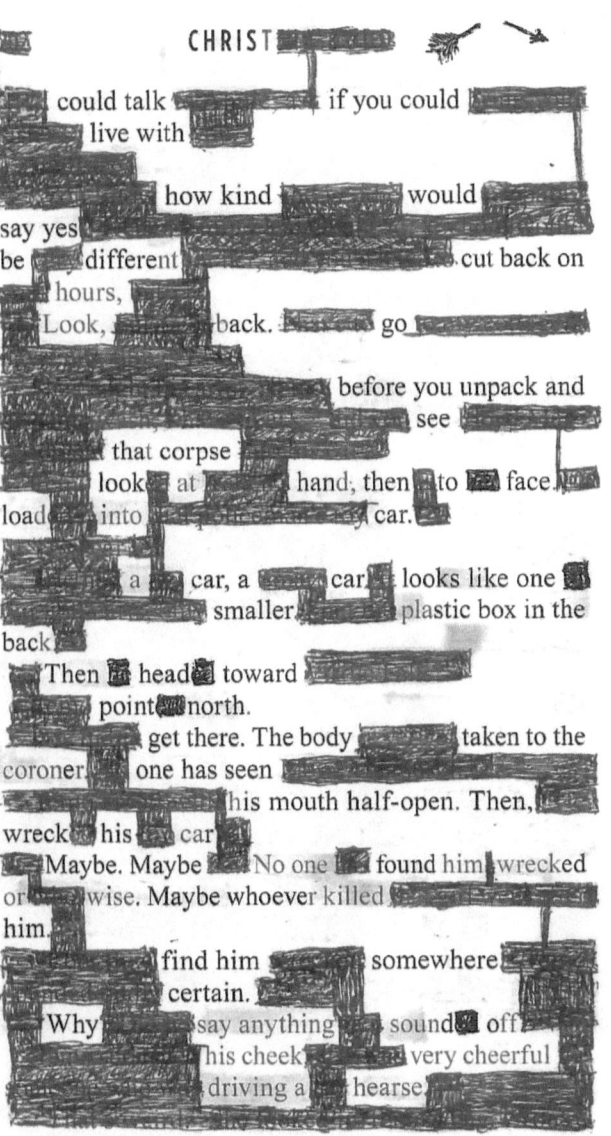

CHRIST

could talk   if you could
live with

          how kind   would
say yes
be   different   cut back on
hours,
Look,   back.   go

                    before you unpack and
                    see
          that corpse
          look   at   hand, then   to   face
load   into   car.

          a   car, a   car   looks like one
                    smaller,   plastic box in the
back
    Then   head   toward
          point   north.
          get there. The body   taken to the
coroner.   one has seen
                    his mouth half-open. Then,
wreck   his   car
    Maybe. Maybe   No one   found him   wrecked
or   wise. Maybe whoever killed
him.
          find him   somewhere
          certain.
    Why   say anything   sound   off
          his cheek   very cheerful
          driving a   hearse

Tonight,

You

see tomorrow.

you

know whether

That

heart

poked through the freezer

a small

hand through the

light

and opened the door,

court evd

? He doesn't

shit about art   but

                    he   says

"She's pretty. Maybe she'll   pay attention.

                              She washed
her hands,

                                                 where
everything is

"Think about it. Someone   used their
hands

                              and
                    their fingers
                    That both amused her and helped convince her

                    This is for

                                                                her

"I like the pilot ███████████████ In and out, ████████████████████████ when the weather's bad ███████████████ but "I'm prejudiced against ██████ the Librarian."

████████████████████████████ but ████

████████████████████████ I would never ████████████

██████████████████████

██████████████████

wave him to silence and ████████████ vanish ████████ with the body. ████████ that would be stupid ████

searching

the long stretches of

possibility   fe-
male

choices

names

into sharp focus.

does that mean

her

her

changed   records

witness

her

winning

entered accepted

I don't think so an ego is online

seen by the world fools everyone.

know her

secrets

the lonely edge of
a past

"What are you escaping?"

tell me

I've never seen

a first
time carefree

that's the game

to seduce
an impulse

but

not attractive

He was so calm, so Zen, everyone stared at him trying to decide if he was serious.

"Frances is dating Mitch, and Mitch said while overseas she provided him more than once from impossible situations. They found out."

"They who?" Mara asked.

"Her team, the people in maintenance, found out that her parents were spies, bred by the government to have superhero powers."

"Wow," Destiny said in an awed voice.

"That's the dumbest thing I've ever heard," Daisy said.

Mara sighed and used the corkscrew to noisily crank the cork out of another bottle of wine.

The oven timer dinged. Xander swooped in, and retrieved the margherita pizza, sliced it and put it in the middle of the coffee table.

Everyone settled down to food, drink and speculation about Kellen Adams, who she really was and where she had come from.

25

"Mr. Giffen, please. Priscilla Gorton's [dead.] Lloyd Magnuson is [disappeared.] [Someone out there] is smuggling something they're willing [to kill for.] Won't you let the government agencies handle this rather than putting your life at risk?" Kellen stood with her hands clasped at her chest, watching Mr. Giffen make himself a cup of oolong tea.

He had returned to his suite [mere moments] before, dressed in military camouflage, chilled to the bone and calm in the face [of] tonight's [failure.] "Miss Adams, I appreciate your concern. But I am not [without] resources. Like you, I've served in the military, and unlike you, I promptly went into security with [a way to] utilize my training. If these smugglers are bringing in illegal and lethal drugs to distribute to our young people, or munitions that they plan to assemble in an act of terrorism, I would [be satisfied] to tell myself, *At least I kept myself safe*." He lifted the tea bag out of his cup and looked inquiringly at her. Politely.

"No, [of course you] wouldn't." Kellen [understood] that

believe

truth

human

find the trust

see a way

Please

promise

to take care

calling
26
times

In the morning, ▓▓▓▓▓ at the house ▓▓▓
▓▓▓▓▓▓▓▓▓▓ her hand moved ▓▓▓▓
▓▓▓▓▓▓▓▓▓ ▓▓▓▓▓▓▓▓▓▓▓▓ She
lifted it to her ear, ▓▓▓▓▓▓▓▓▓▓▓ as ▓▓
the phone rang.

▓▓▓▓▓▓▓▓▓▓▓▓▓▓▓▓▓▓▓▓
▓▓▓▓▓▓▓▓▓▓▓▓▓▓ I got out of the
▓▓▓▓▓▓▓▓▓▓▓▓▓▓▓▓▓ house
and ▓▓▓▓▓▓▓ waited in terror ▓▓▓▓▓

▓▓▓▓▓▓▓▓▓ .'. ▓▓▓▓ Listen, I feel funny
▓▓▓▓▓▓▓▓▓▓▓▓▓▓▓ hunched down
▓▓ and ▓▓▓▓▓▓ concerned ▓▓▓▓ without
saying something. ▓▓▓▓▓▓▓▓
▓▓▓ What is it ▓▓▓ she's doing exactly,
▓▓▓▓▓▓▓▓▓▓

▓▓▓▓ I don't know ▓▓▓▓▓▓
▓▓▓▓▓▓ but I've been spotted behaving oddly.
▓▓▓▓▓▓▓ late at night. ▓▓▓ I'm on fire
for your taking

"Oh no!" Annie whispered. "Not that."

Hastily, Mara said, "I'm not saying she's doing anything wrong. Not a good policy with a guest, of course, but she's handling the resort really well. Especially considering the, you know, body and the way it disappeared with Lloyd Magnuson and all."

Silence from the other end.

"Maybe I shouldn't have said... You did know about the, um, body? Priscilla's body?"

"Leo told me. Not everything, I'm sure, but enough." Annie sounded sorrowful. "I feel awful that my first thought of Priscilla was that she abandoned us. To think the poor child was murdered."

"Yes. The poor child."

"I'm sorry this happened while I was gone."

"Bad timing," Mara agreed. "As to the Kellen thing, I thought you ought to know..."

More silence from the other end.

Mara added, "Maybe I should have kept quiet..."

Annie rallied. "No, dear, thank you for keeping me up-to-date. Of course, that's disappointing to hear. While Kellen's in sole charge of the resort, I'd prefer she concentrate on the job. But these things do happen."

"They do." Mara burst out, "But, Annie, they're out in the middle of the night in the most awful weather, in the cold and dark. I don't know whether it's a romance or something illegal!!"

"Luckily, we have already handled this. Leo and I have sent a second manager to relieve Kellen of this particular problem is, a member of our family, Maximilian

Mara will help! This

said, "Something got delivered for you. A girl. Gorgeous. Lavish. Come on. We're all dying to see who it's from."

Who would send her a present? Why would some-one send her a present?

"Go for it."

and Mara.

in front of the whole world.
employees safe and happy.

This was the kind of treat the troops had loved receiving overseas, luxurious tidbits that reminded them of home and holidays and so far, no one had dropped dead.

Frances ran her finger around the edge of the bowl. "I wonder if this is really a Japanese Awaji piece. If it is, you've got a secret admirer with expensive taste."

The whole secret admirer thing gave Kellen the willies. "I hate that crackle glaze." The decorative bowls at the Greenleaf mansion had sparkled with that glaze, and Erin and Gregory had both adored them. Looking back, Kellen thought it was because they enjoyed the idea of something that was prebroken. Like them. "You take it," she told Frances.

"Really? Okay, I will. Thank you!"

Kellen went back to work unpacking the fruit. Tiny tangerines with their zipper skin smelled like sunshine, summer and citrus. The prickly skin of a fresh pineapple gave off the scent of faraway tropical plantations. Only people who lived where the continual rain bleached the world gray could understand. Kellen lifted one of the last tangerines to her nose, took a long sniff and something long and slim and alive and colorful slithered out of the bowl.

Guests squeaked and screamed and scattered.

By some trick of levitation, Kellen found herself ten feet back from where she'd been.

The snake, ten inches long, with black, gray and red stripes running the length of its body, slid off the table and onto the floor. It moved rapidly across the cool marble toward the front door.

Sheri-Jean moved with intelligence and speed. She dumped the last of the fruit out of the bowl and inverted it over the snake, stopping its escape and the burgeon-

Original

He smiled, a slow signal of delight. "You know me."

Too much delight. Too much anticipation. She briskly freed herself and stepped away. "You look like your uncle. Or like Leo had looked. The same bone—

"Of course. You're right. Leo." He said. "You turned white when you saw that snake. Are you sure you're all right?"

"I don't like snakes. But who does?" A quick glance around the lobby showed all the guests and all the staff standing close to the wall, staring at that bowl as if the snake could somehow escape. "I'm fine. Really, fine."

When Jean was glaring at her, her head tilted, wanting her to snap out of it.

Sheila did. One didn't refuse Sheila Jarvis's demands, spoken or otherwise. In a loud, firm voice, she said, "Let's all go into the lounge, shall we? We'll send the snake to the kitchen to be well washed and our unwelcome visitor can be taken elsewhere. As fast as he's moving toward the door, he must have been late for an appointment."

A little ripple of laughter.

But no one moved.

"Come on, we'll pour some refreshments and give ourselves a chance to relax again." Kellen made a surreptitious shooing gesture to Mara Phillippi and did the dead-tilt glare at Frances.

Mara walked to Max Di Luca, took his arm and smiled into his face. "And you are—?"

Frances ambled toward the lounge, calling, "This calls for a giant bottle of champagne and some fresh-squeezed orange juice. Any excuse for mimosas, I say!"

Carson Lennox offered his arm to Patty and Rin—

two of the Shivering Sherlocks, who were indeed shivering. "Let me help you to a seat."

Now Sheri Jean flashed her evil-supervisor look at her own staff. Desk personnel began to smile, be the kind of hospitality team that helped guests move beyond their shock and back into a vacation state of mind. Soon the lounge was crowded and buzzing with excitement.

The noise died down when a rumpled Nils Brooks stepped into the doorway, pushed his glasses up on his nose and in a bewildered tone asked, "Did I miss something?"

The ███████████████ loud and prolonged, leaving Nils looking confused and the other guests in a much better frame of mind.

Mara returned and took the opportunity to push Kellen around the corner into the lobby. Sheri Jean had disappeared. The snake had disappeared. The bowl sat on the concierge desk. "Thank God for Sheri Jean," Kellen said. "Where do you suppose she took that thing?"

"I don't know and I don't care." In a low, furious voice, Mara said, "That fruit trick was deliberate!"

Brilliant deduction, Mara. "Why do you say that?"

"The doorman didn't recognize the delivery car or driver. There was no card. The fruit was refrigerated, which would have made the snake lethargic until it warmed up and out it popped! Deliberate!"

"I didn't know that. About the doorman." Kellen still felt a little queasy. "Was it Russell? He knows everybody."

"Yes, it was Russell!" Mara's eyes sparked. "Someone has it in for you!"

"The ▓▓▓▓▓▓ was not very nice," Kellen acknowledged.

"Not nice! It was awful. Are you having problems ▓▓▓▓▓▓▓▓▓▓"

"No. Honestly, I don't know who did that." *My dead husband.*

"You don't have ▓▓▓▓▓▓▓▓▓▓ anything. I understand it's embarrassing to be the victim of harassment." Mara glared at Nils Brooks's back. "But ▓▓▓▓▓▓▓▓▓▓▓ and I are glad to help handle any man problems. You say the word."

"Huh? No, it's not him." At once, Kellen realized she had incriminated herself. "I mean, he's not likely. He's a gentle ▓▓▓▓▓ And Kellen was a big fat liar.

"Then who is it?" Mara wanted an answer, and she wanted it now.

Not my dead husband, that's for sure! "Probably a disgruntled guest. We've had some winners over the past few months. Remember the weight lifter who decided he could drop the dumbbell bar and grope your boobs while you spotted him? When you banned him from the gym, he was going to sue for you damaging his marriage?"

"No one has sent me a snake!"

"It wasn't poisonous."

"Get real. Snake. Snake!" Mara flickered her tongue.

Kellen groped in her mind for another memory. "How about this golden oldie? Remember the first week I was here. Remember the drunk lady who didn't chew her food, got a giant piece of steak stuck in her windpipe? I gave her the Heimlich maneuver, dislodged the steak into her boyfriend's soup, and she slammed me against the wall for trying to steal her boy toy?"

Godzilla crush We meet

cupped between

"Call me Max."

Those eyes.

gold intense.

You

"I would do anything for a crisis here. I

fly me up. around

Without saying a word

"Now,

for tonight."

"I suppose we should

move quietly.

all the details.

Max, she said, "We found Lloyd Magnuson. His car was hidden in the foliage at one of the pocket parks along the highway. We *think* from the way it was positioned he pulled into the lot, tried to park, hit the gas instead of the brake and slammed out of the paved area and into the underbrush. Damage done by the last storm, by the winds and the rain, hid the evidence, and it was only this morning that one of my officers found him."

"He's dead," Kellen said.

Sheriff Kwinault paused, her cup halfway to her mouth. "Definitely."

"He hit a tree?" Without asking, Max brought Kellen a mug of hazelnut coffee with sugar.

"An overdose," Sheriff Kwinault answered.

"An overdose!" Kellen gestured to Max.

He closed the office door, then got himself a bottle of water and pulled up another chair.

"Of what?" Kellen asked.

"Before Lloyd Magnuson came to Cape Charade, he was a heroin addict. He got clean, he moved to Cape Charade, he's been clean ever since." Sheriff Kwinault took a sip. "But he had the paraphernalia in the car and there were needle tracks on his arm."

"When I saw him, he was fine," Kellen assured her. "Out of his depth as a law officer, but not impaired."

"What about Priscilla's body?" Max asked.

Sheriff Kwinault put her cup on the desk. "There was no body in the car with him."

"So some kind of foul play," Max said.

Kellen found she needed the coffee; the heat, the caffeine, the sugar alleviated, a little, the chill of death.

"Definitely foul play. No one forced Lloyd to take heroin, but someone had it to offer," Sheriff Kwinault said.

the chill of death.

"Your officers couldn't find him, but someone managed to steal Priscilla's body." Keilen hitched forward in her chair. "How?"

Max reached into his pocket, pulled out a key chain and pushed a button.

His phone squawked.

"I lose my keys all the time," he said. "My wallet, too."

Kellen imagined him coming in from outside and flinging his keys and wallet wherever, and not remembering where they had landed. That evening, he would cook dinner, talk about his day, sing, play cards, laugh...

The next morning, when he got ready to leave for work, he couldn't find his keys and wallet, and he roared and fussed as if someone had stolen his belongings, when it was his own carelessness at fault...

It was almost as if she had been there.

He continued, "I've got a finder on them, and it's the least sophisticated of the electronics. All the killer had to do was tape a finder on the lid of the plastic box, and he or she could find the body in no time flat."

"Law enforcement gets easier and harder all the time," Sheriff Kwinault said. "Who saw him last?"

"Temo." Kellen knew Temo; with his mother's history, he didn't use, sell or tolerate drug use, but he did recognize it when he saw it. While she made the call on speakerphone, Sheriff Kwinault gestured to Max to be quiet.

He stood and paced over to the window.

Temo answered, sounding tired and distracted.

"I have the sheriff here," Kellen said. "They found Lloyd Magnuson."

Temo's voice changed to wary. "He's dead?"

"Very dead." Sheriff Kwinault tinkered with her cup. Can you tell me about it?"

"Start at when I left you with him and the body," Kellen said.

Temo waited a moment, maybe to gather his thoughts. "I told Kellen I'd clean up the girl's bones, so Kellen left. The policeman, he didn't want to touch anything. He really didn't want to touch the girl, so he got in contact with the resort and asked for a plastic box to put her in, then he left in an ATV to get it. He was gone for a while."

"How long a while?" Sheriff Kwinault asked.

"I had collected the bones, all the bits of cloth, and I said a prayer for the repose of her soul. So…half an hour? A little more?"

"Thank you. That helps," Sheriff Kwinault said. "When Lloyd Magnuson returned…?"

"He was driving his toy car. He had a big square plastic bin, like a storage bin where you keep a child's toys. I put the girl's bones in there."

"How was Lloyd?" Sheriff Kwinault's tone was carefully neutral.

Temo's tone matched hers. "I don't know what you mean."

"Was he sad for the death?" Kellen asked. "Did he seem frightened of the remains?" The caffeine and sugar helped her remember the scene, to get past her own horror and focus on the memory of Lloyd Magnuson at that moment.

"Most people don't like the idea of driving with a corpse," Kellen said.

iff Kwinault said. "Assuming Temo was telling the truth—

"He isn't a seller," Kellen said fiercely.

"—Lloyd Magnuson came back to get Priscilla Carter's body and he was already stoned. As he drove, he got progressively less able to operate the car, tried to stop somewhere, drove into the bush and out of sight. He died there, and at some point, someone took the plastic container with the corpse out of the vehicle." Sheriff Kwinault leaned forward. "Why was there a corpse with no hands? Why was Lloyd Magnuson given drugs? Why was the body stolen? What is going on here?"

Max answered, "Someone is using the Yearning Sands dock for smuggling."

Good. Kellen hadn't had to anguish over how much to tell Sheriff Kwinault. Max had taken the issue out of her hands.

Sheriff Kwinault was patently not surprised. "Do we know what? Or who?"

"We don't know what's being smuggled," Max said.

Kellen didn't correct him.

Max continued, "But we do think the head of smuggling is someone here at the resort."

"Very likely it's drugs, and whoever gave Lloyd the heroin is our felon." Sheriff Kwinault looked at Kellen. "You say not Temo?"

"No." Yet he needed to support his sister, and he'd do anything for her. Kellen feared he could be desperate enough to join a ruthless smuggler. Why not suspect him of distributing heroin, too? "Maybe."

"Any other suspects?" Sheriff Kwinault asked.

"I think too many." Max looked at Kellen for confirmation.

She nodded.

Sheriff Kwinault sighed. "Have you called the Coast Guard?"

"Yes," Kellen said. "That is, not me, but yes, they've been contacted."

"Then they're keeping an eye on things here in between other duties." Sheriff Kwinault tapped her fingers on the desk. "Let me talk to them. The fact we've got a mutilated body that's missing and a dead law officer should get their attention."

"Will they listen to you?" Kellen asked.

"Yes. I'm the former Virtue Falls Coast Guard commander." Sheriff Kwinault gestured at the star on her chest. "And I have this. Semper."

Max indicated Kellen. "She's a veteran of a war zone."

"Really?" Sheriff Kwinault looked Kellen over. "I wouldn't have guessed. Keeping up with your fitness?"

Kellen thought of Mara and their daily sparrings. "Yes." Like she had a choice.

"With any luck, our smugglers will underestimate you." Sheriff Kwinault stood. "I'll send officers to check in every few hours. Call us for any reason, no matter how small. Max, you're working security for the duration?"

"I am."

"Good. You look big. You look scary. Maybe that'll keep the bad guys at bay until the Coast Guard can scoop them up."

"I'll do my best Incredible Hulk imitation," Max promised.

Sheriff Kwinault smirked at him. "You're closer to the giant Marshmallow Man."

Yes. They had obviously met before.

Kellen and Sheriff Kwinault shook hands again.

"Can I offer you a ride into a restaurant before you go?" Kellen asked.

"Thank you. I'd be delighted to take you up on it, but the weather folks are predicting a big storm and I'm on duty." Sheriff Kwinault shrugged her way into her coat, "Not that the weather folks have been right very often this winter."

"Dinner to go?" Kellen asked.

"That would be much appreciated," Sheriff Kwinault conceded.

"I'll set her up," Max said and took Sheriff Kwinault to the elevator and the lobby.

While he was gone, Kellen texted Mr. Gilfilen the news of Lloyd Magnuson's death and ended with a plea that he cease his operation.

His text came back. Acknowledged.

By which he meant he had received her news, and he would continue to do what he thought right.

When Max came back, Kellen was staring out the big window, where the everlasting gray clouds churned and threatened. "I gave Frances instructions to give Kateri anything she wanted as a to-go meal."

"Thank you."

"I called Annie and Leo to tell them about Lloyd Magnuson."

"Thank you again." She hadn't even thought to do that. "I informed Mr. Gilfilen. You do know about Mr. Gilfilen?"

"Leo told me. I think it's a stupid idea, but Vince Gilfilen is a force to be reckoned with." Max watched her watch the sky and asked, "Are you okay?"

"Somehow, that was worse than I expected." Kate found she was sitting ramrod straight, her fists clenched at her sides. "I don't want to think of Lloyd being tempted by a devil. It's cruel and callous, and whoever it is, whatever it is, is here at the resort."

"At your refuge."

"Yes."

"And whoever did this could be your friend."

"Yes." The word was no more than a sigh.

He came around the desk and knelt beside her chair, and made his offer with every evidence of sincerity. "It's dangerous here. If you'd like to go away, I can assume control."

Shocked, she looked him square in the face. "What? What are you talking about?"

"I'll talk to Annie. I'm capable of being resort assistant manager. You can go on vacation, take a leave of absence. No one would think the worse of you. This situation is dangerous and—"

She pushed her chair away from him. "I can't leave. Run away? The resort is my responsibility. The people here are my responsibility. If one of my friends is guilty of these heinous acts—well, I recommended them to Annie and Leo. What kind of person would I be if I ran away?" She would be Cecilia, running away from her cousin's death.

"I thought—"

"Stop thinking. You're security until Mr. Griffith returns to his regular duties, that's all. I'm in charge of the resort. I'll stay in charge of the resort." She stood up. "Now if you'll excuse me, I need to make rounds, talk to the guests and employees, assure them everything is being handled to the best of our abilities and their

Do the Thing

thing— meet
talk

stride out

This was expected.

do the

30

Real Terrors

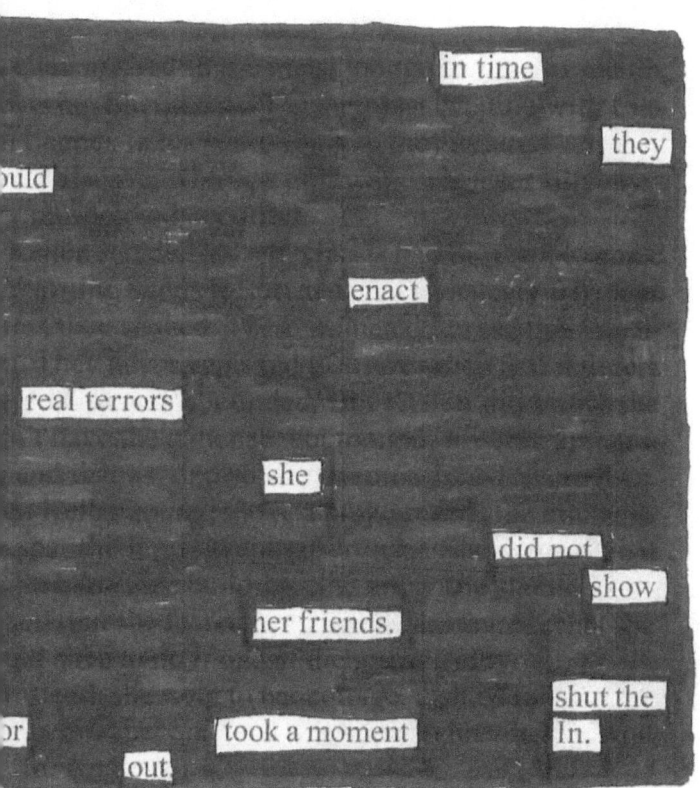

in time

they

ould

enact

real terrors

she

did not

show

her friends.

shut the
In.

or

took a moment

out,

alone in a place

no
constant

ev-
sounded

erything
easy,

in the middle of

water

panic

remember how

She didn't

slash

her
fingers

elevated

voices.

forced
quiescent,
alone...

Pale green
leafy tree   gray
sky.
music

The door was
            metal
                                    facedown
        on a tray   was
            applesauce.
    the other side of   shiny chrome
                        God
            was keeping her drugged.

                    She remembered

    adrenaline   fury,
                                            Blood
Pain

    her elbow
                            Her neck
    Every muscle

                            her chest
                        with fingernails

31

That day, ██████████████████████████████
██
a skeleton crew ████████████████████████████
██████████████ was taking some much needed downtime.
████████████████████████████████████

A park, trees bare of leaves, openmouthed pedestrians running. ██████████████████████
████████████████████████████████
██████████████

In the background, a man raced toward them and...
██████████████████████████████ ...was gone.

████████████████████████████
████████████████████████████
████████████████████████████
████████████████████████████
████████████████████████████
██████████████████
████████████████

hear, because by their body language and by logic, she
could anticipate their needs.

She had never had this gift before, but she knew
how to use it now.

They put the paperwork in front of her. She filled
it all in without hesitation, using Kellen's New York
address, Kellen's birthday, Kellen's degrees. She was,
she realized, being Kellen Rae Adams in every way.
She got ready to sign and date the forms. "What day
is this?" she asked.

Sergeant Barnes said, "May twelfth."

Then she scrawled Kellen's signature and passed
over the paperwork.

The recruiter ran through it all, asked a few ques-
tions, got to the end and laughed, scratched out the date
and passed it back. "I know—I still get the year wrong,
too. Initial the change, then we're on to the next stage."

That was when she discovered she'd lost more than
a year of her life.

Lost it, apparently, forever.

Someone knocked on her front door.

She clutched the arms of her chair. She knew who
was there.

Another knock. The bell rang.

"Bastard." She stood and clattered down the spiral
stairs. She looked through the peephole, then flung open
the door. "What a surprise," she said in a voice heav-
ily laden with irony.

Nils Brooks stood on the porch. "May I come in?"
Like a vampire who had to be invited to cross the
threshold.

"If you must." She backed away.

He dusted a few flakes of snow off his shoulders.

There, in the porch light, his disguise was stripped away. He looked like a dangerous man, strong, wiry, with a determined jaw and a fake pair of eyeglasses in his pocket. He came in, flung off his Burberry coat and hung it on the rack. "The weathercasters got it wrong again. The main thrust of the storm went south to Oregon."

She didn't answer, and she didn't turn up her lights.

His conversational tone changed. "What do you know?" He demanded information as if he was in charge.

"Lloyd Magnuson is dead."

He dismissed the information with a wave of the hand. "We already had that figured out. What else do you know?"

"You don't give a damn, do you?" She looked at him in the dim light and saw a man driven by ambition. "Someone trapped Lloyd Magnuson by using his own weakness and now he's dead."

He seated himself in the easy chair beside her front door. "Gossip at the resort says he used heroin."

"Exactly."

"Then why was he trapped? He was simply weak." Nils couldn't have sounded more indifferent.

"I don't like you." She had never meant anything so much. "Do you have no weaknesses?"

"Yes." He came to his feet, caught her shoulders and kissed her.

She didn't punch him in the ribs or use the serrated edge of her flashlight on his face. She let him kiss her, mouth to mouth, breath to breath, and as the moment stretched out, she relaxed, accepted the sensation, lived in the moment... and when he lifted his mouth from hers, she said, "I'd give it a B plus."

"Are you frigid?"

stretched out on his back. The throw rug was rolled and thrust under his neck, tilting his head back, revealing a dark throat bruised darker in a long thin line. Someone had used a garrote on him.

The cat, the mangy cat he had rescued, sat on the counter and growled at her.

"It's all right," she told it. "I'll help him." She stepped over his prone body, faced the door, dropped on her knees beside him. "Mr. Gilfilen!" She touched his cheek.

His eyelids flickered. He twitched as if fighting for breath, but his chest didn't move. She adjusted his head, pinched his nose, put her mouth to his and tried to fill his lungs. No luck.

The swelling in his throat had obstructed his airway.

She had no time, and she had no choice. If he didn't get oxygen soon, he would die, another victim of the Librarian.

Kellen would not stand for that. She understood the procedure for an emergency tracheotomy. She knew how…in theory.

She'd learn on the job. Right now. As she opened the first aid kit, she called Max. He answered, she said, "Nine-one-one to the west wing. STAT."

"On my way." He hung up.

She searched the first aid kit, found gauze, tape, a tube. Nothing to cut with. Very well. She popped open her pocketknife. It was sharp; she always made sure of that. But she had no time to sterilize. Hell, she didn't have time to think.

The cat growled again.

"I'm hurrying," she said. With her fingers, she located Mr. Gilfilen's Adam's apple, found the spot between it and the next hard ring, and without pausing for-nightmares

shook a killer

33

The official story was

dark and suspicious   -and

                                        damned shady,

the other resorts, reassuring the guests. More than that, he was the security manager, he was clearly packing a firearm and he was *visible*. His size alone, packaged nicely in that dark suit, seemed to reassure everyone and keep terror at bay.

Kellen personally arranged transportation for those headed to the airstrip and organized the farewell appetizers and beverages in the lobby for every departing guest. Finding the necessary staff to handle the workload proved the real challenge; most of the spa staff called in sick or scared, some of the maids and desk staff simply didn't come to work and the security center was unmanned. Chef Reinhart and Chef Norbert arrived separately, both bearing well-sharpened butcher knives in their belts; the sous chef for each was a no-show. That created a great kerfuffle in the kitchen as they shouted commands at each other, until Gabriella got tired of listening and made them chop for her.

Birdie drove the first group to the airstrip to catch Chad Griffin's plane to Seattle, but when Kellen tried to locate Temo for the second shift, he was unreachable, and she wanted to find him, shake him, make him be the Temo she believed him to be.

The last group out the door was the Shivering Sherlocks; they were scheduled to check out today anyway, but Kellen gave them a voucher for one night free on their next visit and got into the driver's seat to take them to the airstrip. Mitch came along to serve the food and drink, and to charm the women with his good looks and flattery.

That was fine with Kellen. Her focus kept wandering, running through the suspects in her mind. To pick up a gun and shoot someone required a cold purpose—

or a hot temper. But to deliberately attempt to strangle a man, to watch him kick and struggle, then when he was subdued, to take a sharp blade and try to sever his hand...that was cold. That was vicious.

Mr. Gilfilen had lived, but what had he done to his attacker to escape? He couldn't tell her. He couldn't tell anyone. He was unconscious, recovering from surgery, fighting for his life. She would figure this out, and she would get her revenge. For Mr. Gilfilen, and for all of the victims who had died for this deadly game of smuggling. She would get revenge for herself, too. She'd come back to the United States determined to work hard, play hard, be strong, be brave for all the days that were left to her. Not to witness more pain. Not to fight an unseen foe who lived for blood and cruelty.

Who was it?

She glanced at Mitch, half-turned toward the back, asking the Shivering Sherlocks about their mystery weekend, asking what they would remember when they got home.

"I'll tell you what I'll remember." Candy sat directly behind the driver's seat, and she leaned forward and spoke right in Kellen's ear. "The guest bath in Carson Lennex's penthouse was busy, so I hustled upstairs to his suite to use the potty up there. Guess what I found?"

"Tell me you didn't dig through his nightstand and find his porn," Rita said.

"Not porn." In the rearview mirror, Kellen saw Candy frown. "I don't think. It certainly wasn't hidden away."

Nancy leaned forward out of the very back seat. "What was it?"

Candy said, "He had these stone statues on glass

September."

caught

along the

stories

Of

September

smuggling

sleep

caught

art and

trouble

34

██████ Kellen ██████████████████████████████ shelf.
████ missing one.

The last piece of the collection is a ██████████
from the tomb wall. Very rare find. Christine's mouse
knuckled in fossil. Most Mayans wrote on paper rather
than ██████ the wild fig tree.

Kellen widened her eyes at him.

And you do ██████ the statue and so forget
I studied ██ don't read Mayan hieroglyphs with ██
█████████████████████████████ curse, and
██████████████████ to ███████ tormented
by ██████ dead Mayan lord, so I returned it to the ███
███ too.

The ██ things are going. I don't know will you ██
forced █████████ tough. So much federal bureaucra-
█████████████████ the ship? I've ██ ██ to Ma's for
safekeeping ███ not one worry ██ ██ ██
of course, how ██ the parcel they come in. He

"Who is Nils Brooks?" he asked. "Who is he *really*?"

Should she tell him? Annie had sent her trusted nephew as security for the resort. But death stalked the dim corridors and windswept grounds. Kellen needed help and Max could give it, and so in the plainest, fastest way she could, she outlined her history with Nils.

When she finished, Max said, "The CIA? The MFAA? He's *undercover*? Come on! You do realize how absurd that all sounds?"

"I do, especially in light of his disappearance. But, Max, right now, I only trust me and thee, and I'm not so sure about thee. Or me, for that matter." She meant that more than she could say. About both of them.

But he chuckled, a nice, rich, warm sound. "I'll help you search. You think he's here—"

"He is not leaving now, not when things are coming to a head."

"Where can he be that we can't see him?"

Her annoyance with Nils fought with her fear for him. "Dead under a rock on the beach."

"Kellen, with all due respect, I can hardly believe he's former CIA and undercover with a newly re-formed government agency that is concerned with, of all things, antiquities."

Everything Max said fed into her own doubts, made her feel foolish and resentful. "If there's a chance that he's telling the truth—"

"I know. You're right. Re-forming the MFAA is a good idea. I simply don't know that I believe the government ever follows through on good ideas." Max pushed his hair off his forehead. "Where is he if he's not dead under a rock?"

"In the spa. In the restrooms. In one of the guest

rooms. Because of privacy issues, there are no security cameras in those locations."

"I'll check the spa first," Max said in heavy irony.

"I'm going to check his cottage. He didn't answer the house phone this morning when we wanted him to evacuate. He didn't respond when Frances knocked on his door. She said she went in and called for him and searched. But she's frightened. I can't see her poking into every corner."

"You think he hid in the closet or behind the shower curtain?" Max's tone started out incredulous and ended in a brief, humorous laugh.

"Or he was out beating the bushes."

"Or he's dead somewhere." Max said that in a matter-of-fact tone.

"Yes. That's possible, too. I texted him and he never answered."

"Be careful out there," Max said.

"Be careful in here," Kellen replied.

"No problem. I'm the Incredible Hulk, remember?"

"And I'm Wonder Woman."

As she started to walk out, he caught her arm. "After this is over, we'll need to talk."

She took a breath. "Philadelphia?"

"You remember?"

Her heartbeat sped up. *Confirmation.* He was part, maybe all, of her forgotten past. "Not really."

Heat shimmered in the air between them. They looked at each other, each searching for some remnant of the past, of passion remembered and passion forgotten.

"Later," he said and let her go.

There might not be a body,

If she did believe him chest rising and falling desperate

her hands arms, neck,

So she turned a touch into a shadow, a restless ocean without self.

some parts of her body didn't care

"Um, can you let go

"Right." The rumble of and he released her reluctantly.

to go No

She slipped and then rs...

bitterly cold wind whipped swirled

After I left

I couldn't see

the clouds were low
roaring

pressed to his black eye. '

maybe
ready to listen.

running   head down,

pleased   that—

It was *dark*.

Heavy box, took them both to lift it. N_ I couldn't iden-
tify them, either."

"But you could see them."

"I had my night vision by then. _ I was wonder-
ing what the hell I was doing ther_ _ecause th_
a st_ _ _ission. I had in_ _ _ _ _ _ _ey
h_ _ _ _ _ _ _ _ _ _ _ _ _ _ _tter they
_ _ _ _ _ _ _ _ _ _ _ _ _ _ at I wasn't a

_ _ _ _ _ _ _ asn't an ap-
_ _ _ _ _ _ live, so she
coul_

_ _ _ _ _ _ignaled, and
the t_ _ _ _ _ _ _ _ _ _ _hed
into_ _ _ _ cockroaches _ _ _ _ _ _nt"
_ _ _ _ _ _ _ _ _e. The _ _ _ _ldn't
h_

_ _ _ _ _ _ _ _ t that
_ _ _ _box _ _ _ _there,
_ _ _ _ _ _ make

_ _ _ _ _ _ _ d answer,
_ _ _ _ _ence. _ I k_ _ _ _ere horny
_ _ _ _ _ _ _thinking."

_ _ _ _ _ing with the s_ _ _ rat_ _ happens.
_ _ _ _ _ _ _ _ ding it did, to _ _ _gged _ box over
to _ _ _ TV, _ _ _ged the se_ _ _ _rned m_ _culptured
a vertebra lifting it up an_ _ _ the storage bin and
dropped the seat over it _ _ _ _bout the time the shout-
ing started. He watch_ _ _ _ for a few moments. "You
don't want to say a word about what could have hap-
pened next, do you? You're afraid to feed me informa-
tion, lead the witness."

know how it is. You're fighting, you get hurt, it's dark, might be the enemy, might be friendly fire."

"Why didn't you stay with him? He almost expired before I got there."

"He called you, then he had me stretch him out on the bathroom floor with that rug under his neck. He was pretty pissed, and so was I, and I thought he would be fine until you got there. So I went out searching for the bad guys. I figured they had to be somewhere on the resort grounds." Nils grinned savagely. "I didn't find them, but I found the right ATV. Still warm, and the box was still under the seat. They drove those artifacts back to the resort for me."

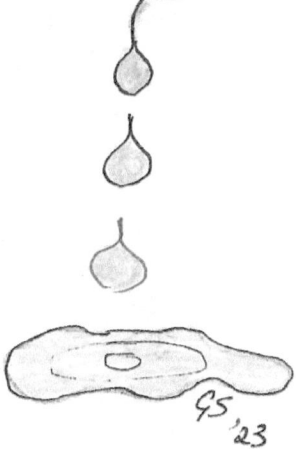

35

Kellen laughed in delight. "Did you get the box out and put it somewhere safe?"

He lifted his elbow. "Couldn't."

"So we don't know what's in it or where it is now?"

"Not really, but unless by sheer chance they figured out where I hid it, it's still somewhere on the property in an ATV."

She stared at him in admiration. "You have balls of steel."

Without an ounce of modesty, he said, "I do, don't I?"

"Where was the ATV parked?"

"By the maintenance garage."

Kellen felt the blood drain from her face, felt the clammy chill cover her skin. "So maybe one of my people."

"Not proof. But likely."

Temo? Mitch? Adrian?… Birdie? Tears pricked at her eyes. She didn't want to know one of her friends, her team, had joined the dark side. She wanted to believe in them. Now she doubted all of them.

Nils watched her, analyzed her. "You face every chal-you

slipped

into

opposition   taking

care   They don't care
if they kill every person

all they want

to do is get

kissed her nevertheless,

in   dark and   after

36

released

climb

a burst of sound   shout

cry

slam

bleeding

at the door

sister

Without hesitation
do
do

live

Wealthy collectors paid him to destroy history and sell it to them. He made money. He killed his people to assure their cooperation. He cut off their hands. She had believed that Nils Brooks had been hurt helping Mr. Gilfilen. What a joke. He'd been hurt attacking Mr. Gilfilen. *Nils Brooks* was the Librarian.

As she drove toward the resort, she called the security center.

The connection crackled and failed.

She didn't believe this was a natural outage. Not tonight. Rain fell, but this wasn't a big storm, this wasn't numbing cold, blasting wind or sleet. This was far too convenient. Someone had sabotaged the resort's communications network. The CB radio in Annie's office would work to call in outside help—but she didn't have time to wait.

As she drove, she planned her rescue of Carson Lennex. She needed help. She needed someone at her back, so she veered for the maintenance garage. She used her pass card to open the door and stuck her head in. Lights were on, but dim. So the electricity was out and everything was running on generator. One of the resort's working pickup trucks, a Ford F-250 crew cab, sat over the hydraulic lift, waiting to be raised and its oil changed. From the back of the shop, she heard the clink of tools. "Birdie!" she called. "Grab your pistol and your Kevlar vest. I need your help!"

No answer.

She frowned and stepped inside. "Birdie?"

Someone gave a muffled scream. A warning.

Kellen dived to the floor, aiming for the pickup, skidding along the concrete.

A bullet slammed into the door where she'd been standing. She'd walked into an ambush.

She low-crawled to the pickup and took cover under it. Silence.

Where was Birdie? That was her scream, Kellen knew. Who was shooting?

Who was capable of disabling the communications network?

The same guy who had *fixed* the last outage. Mitch. Mitch was working for the Librarian.

She unsnapped her side holster, click-released the safety on her pistol, slid it back in place.

What had he done to Birdie? She was hurt, maybe dying. She needed help, and only Kellen could get it for her.

"Mitch, this is stupid." Kellen spoke calmly, persuasively, while with all her stealth, she slid along the floor, keeping well under the protection of the vehicle, moving from her current position to one closer to the back of the shop, trying to figure out a strategy. A tool chest stood there, great for defensive positioning. Lots of metal, lots of tools inside. On wheels, but nobody ever moved a filled tool chest easily. "This can't end well for you."

From the back wall, she heard Mitch's soft laugh. "No, Captain, it can't end well for *you*. I've got orders to eliminate you. You know too much. You see too much." Reflectively, he added, "I did say you would be a problem."

He walked forward, his boots smacking the concrete and echoing around the steel-frame structure. She knew without looking he had his firearm out, grasped in both hands, pointed at the pickup. She also knew where he

He walked   his
pistol   gaze pointed down. Like

targets.   swung her weight
    at his abdomen.
Six feet.

            suckered.
        shot. Missed. Damn   left hand!
Seven feet.
        full extension.   ground to a halt
        exposed, hanging   like a piñata.

            Blew a hole in his thigh.
        went wide.   in agony, crum-
pled
        hit his chest
impact   square
        onto his back.   he
            raised   red-rimmed eyes to
her, supported his gun hand   and
aimed.
    She prepared to drop, knowing she could never out-
run a bullet
    From above.
                knocking him flat.
unconscious.

                    spilled out,
thick, heavy,   paper and *weight.*
                        "Take that, you bas-
tard." Her voice   a croak.

She landed

ing a pool

right hand left hand

Still underestimated.

pushed

off the wall and

turned

so fast

God screamed

~~Then, ruthlessly practical,~~ she reloaded her pistol, ~~placed it in her holster~~. ~~As backup, she found his fire-~~ ~~arm~~ and stored it in her boot.

~~She had~~ no ~~way to call for~~ help, no time ~~to find Max~~ ~~for help~~. She was alone.

37

Kellen ~~ran out into the silent night, where black streamers of clouds~~ clawed ~~across~~ the sky, grasping the stars, ~~then releasing them~~. She ~~climbed into her ATV and drove toward the castle~~, toward ~~Carson Lennex's tower room~~, where light radiated like a beacon. ~~Time and~~ worry oppressed her, ~~and the taste of~~ grim fear filled her ~~mouth~~.

~~After such a delay, after so much time spent suffering under Nils Brooks's hands~~, was Carson Lennex even alive?

She ~~let herself in a side entrance~~, ran the dim, silent corridors ~~toward the elevators that led~~ to the private suites. ~~She pushed the up button.~~

~~Nothing moved. Nothing lit.~~

A step behind her ~~had her~~ pulling her pistol ~~and~~ spinning around.

Sheri Jean ~~stood~~ like a ~~disconsolate~~ ghost. "~~Everything's~~ broken. ~~The elevators, the intercoms, the house phones. Some of the lights are running on generator.~~

from

there

She

used   to enter

the dark

loaded with   lace

"Could it ever   be easy?"

curse her

Hurry. No time.

there it was,

an ancient

silver fork

IN

useless

with age.

slid down,

in

ungreased anguish.

an archaic

grinding

she could see

it.

looked sturdy

She couldn't

think

of

Her pistol

Light

her

inside

faint

torture

opening   of
chest

She

swelled,

screamed   This   moment.

rocked   and

grasped

KM

he tried to call 911. He had no cell service. He tried to text. Nothing. "Damn it." When he was running around looking for Nils Brooks, someone had cut the resort's ties to the outside world. Probably Nils Brooks.

In the hallway, he heard the female begin to cry. He crawled out of the closet, and as he untied her, he said, "He's alive. What's your name?"

"I'm Destiny Longacre. I work here."

He remembered her photo from resort records. "As a masseuse, right? Can you tell me what happened?"

"I came in this morning. Came in the outer spa door. It was open a little. I thought, *I didn't do it. Someone's going to get in trouble. I hope it's not me.* I got inside, into the hall for the treatment rooms, and I saw something splattered on the floor. Mara hates when the spa is dirty. She insists we clean everything before we leave. She's really weird about it, so I thought we'd missed something and I'd clean up before she came in. I got the carpet cleaner and started on the splatter, and the towel came out red and I couldn't figure out what..." She gasped, trying to get a breath between the tears. "Then I thought, *it's blood.* I looked up, and she was standing in the door of one of the treatment rooms."

"She?"

"Mara Philippi. Our boss. She was beat-up, bruises on her face, blood at the corner of her lip—I thought she'd been attacked. I thought whoever was attacking people had attacked her."

Max knew then. He pulled out his phone and tried to text Kellen. Nothing. He tried to call. No connection.

Destiny continued, "I jumped up and said, *Are you okay?* and she pointed a gun at me and said, *Clean it up.* She's said it before, lots of times, but never with a

gun. I was like, ~~Mom, with Destiny!~~ She laughed, ~~sort
of crazy~~, and said, *That's for sure*."

"~~I freed~~ her hands and feet. He gestured toward
~~Xander, unconscious~~ in the closet. "~~Did she shoot him?~~"

"~~Then not~~ she hit him. Xander came ~~in, and she~~ told
him to ~~wake up, and~~ he was, ~~he really was. But he~~
~~was all Xander-like, talking to~~ her ~~about~~ Karma and
~~nonviolence and~~ the way ~~of the~~ ~~Dalai Lama~~, and she
~~just up and bonked him~~ on the head with ~~the butt~~ of
her gun. He ~~fell down and I~~ screamed ~~and I thought she~~
~~was going to shoot me, but I couldn't stop~~ screaming."
Destiny w~~iped~~ her nose on the ~~sleeve of~~ her ~~sweater~~.
"~~The children were like~~ so cute ~~I~~ like him ~~a lot. I~~
thought he was going ~~to save me~~. But he went ~~right up~~
to M~~om and told~~ her G~~ramma Jenney had the statues~~."

~~"The statues?"~~

"~~That's what~~ he said. I don't know w~~hat it means~~, but
he said G~~ramma Jenney had the statues, and so~~ ~~now~~
she was in ~~his suite to let Mitch in, and Mitch would~~
~~cut~~ electricity and ~~communication~~s."

Again ~~Mitch~~ tried ~~to escape and call. Mitch had~~ done as
~~he was~~ told. C~~ommunications were down~~.

~~While he tried, Destiny did all the rest, and~~ she ~~Mom~~
told him *Good job* ~~as she picked up and stash[ed] as ... in ...~~
~~the ...~~, and she left and he ~~did. He told me she~~ tried to
escape h~~er, and I will ... she~~ huddled on the floor and
r~~ubbed her wrists~~. ~~My fingers are tingling. I hope he~~
did~~n't ruin my hands. I have to work today. I need~~
~~the money!~~

~~She~~ was in shock. M~~om wrapped~~ a blanket ~~around her~~
should~~ers. The~~ resort w~~ill compensate you~~ for lost time.
~~The paramedics will check you over. Your hands are okay~~

and Xander, too." Although how he was going to contact them, he didn't know. He stood. "Can you let them in?"

Her teeth were chattering, but she nodded. "What *wrong* with Mara?" she asked urgently.

He hurried toward the door. "Mara Philippi is the Librarian."

"A librarian? No, she's illiterate."

He swiveled on his heel. "*What?*"

Patiently, Destiny explained. "She can't read."

"She has to be able to read. She runs a very successful business."

"She doesn't tell anybody. I figured it out for myself. She uses the computer accessibility settings as a work-around. She's got it all worked out."

"Holy shit." Somehow, knowing that made Mara, the Librarian, so much creepier. He moved out of the suite and into the stairwell. It was going to have to be a fast run up those eight stories to Carson Lennex's suite, but he had to make it.

He'd been too late once before. He wouldn't be too late now.

I finally

knew

straight. Mara her p

jagged

thin

free.

with a gymnast's speed and grace.

touch

her hand and

This was it:

oblivion s

merciful

e nothing but

that moment.

A light came on.

"I d

didn't have breath.   only her lips moved...

Taking her time,
drawing out
Deliberately, she p

had to   *had to.*

everything
blurred, overlapped.

She was i
She was i

going
to m

going
to n

to crunch it back in place. It was still broken, but as the joint slid back into place, the relief was immediate.

"Your legs?" Max insisted.

That took more concentration, but at last she shifted her feet, pulling them toward her, then using them to leverage herself into a sitting position.

He watched, offering no assistance, and if ever a man showed terror, it was him. She knew why. He feared she had survived, only to live a life without dance, without speed, without motion. Unlike hers, his memory of her time spent unconscious and recovering in the hospital would be whole and unbearable. He feared history was repeating itself.

"I'm not paralyzed." She put her bruised and broken hand to her shattered chest. "I am in a lot of pain. Do you have an aspirin on you?"

He sighed in relief. "Stay still. Stay quiet. We'll get a helicopter here to lift you out." He pulled out his phone, tried to dial and swore virulently. "Someone put some kind of damper on the system."

"Mitch did it." She took a breath. "Birdie killed Mitch. And I did."

Carson said, "I don't know much about electronics, but I know where the server center is and I can try to figure out how Mitch sabotaged it." He moved like a man who'd been bound and tortured, like a man in pain. But his eyes sparked, his forehead scowled, his mouth sneered and, at the same time, gave the tiniest twist of pain. Kellen could see why the man had won his Academy Awards. He knew how to express emotion, and he knew the right emotion to express.

"There's a CB radio in Annie's office," Kellen said.

"I know ███████████████████████████

███████████ "What's wrong ████████?"

████████████████████████████

████████████ he's too wonderful to lose." ████

████████████████████████████

████████████████████████████

████████████████ "Let's see what we can do with this." █████████████████████

"Better," ██he whispered.

████████████████████████████

████████████████████████████

████████

██████████ that sense of being in two places returned: ████████████████████
████████████ the blank nothingness of…of what?

"Kellen?" ████████████████████ "Ceecee?"

█"No." Panic ████████████ ██he wasn't Ceecee. ██he wasn't Cecilia. ██he could never be Cecilia again. Those flashes of moments past…they were not memories. They were merely impressions. ████████████

████████████████████████████

████████████████████████████

████████████████████████████

████████████████████████████

"I'm fine," she said.

"Oh?"

"Well. Solid

"Let me see."

off wrists. He worked the vest's fasteners free,

protective embrace.

t. Why she cared, she didn't know. Yet it seemed unfair

. It made her half-remembered

dreams seem pitiful,

"Oh, Ceecee…"

she corrected him. "Kellen."

radiated from the center of her chest, and it was growing.

regain her dignity, her strength,

"It stops death.

G R R

he crawled

                                    slowly
                poised   re
        if he fell.

                                    bones
                    moving, grinding.
    He.   resented
            his
                left hand
it fit   awkwardly,

                                                his ha

                    prayed to God
        for   you.
                        he wanted to
couldn't.

                        he could only
            call   "   I need you."

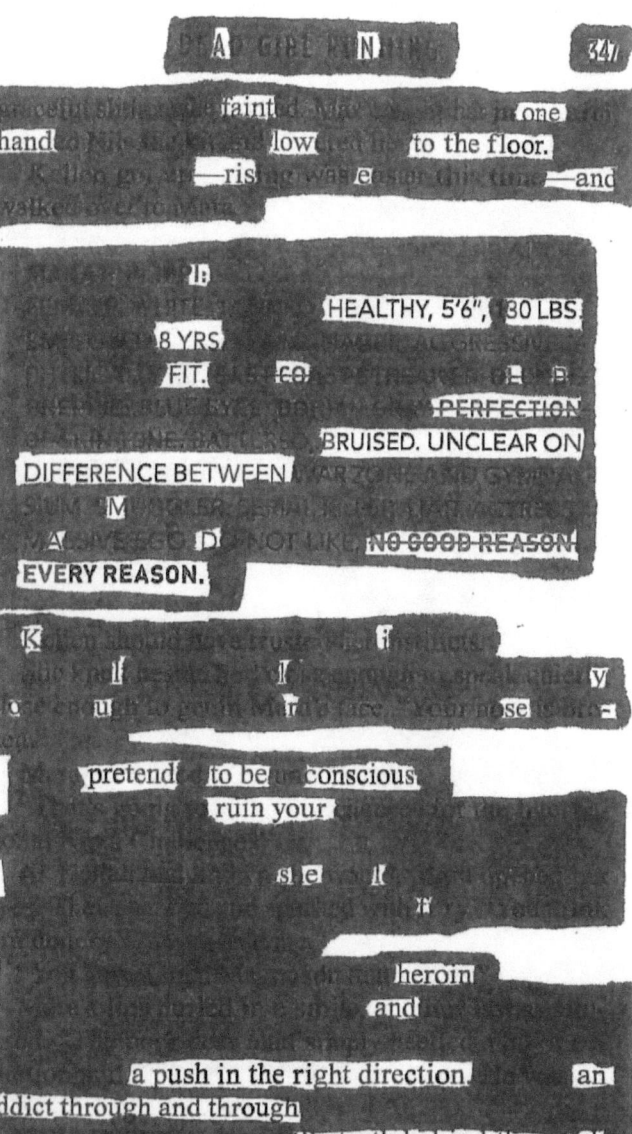

...ceful shrug... ...fainted. Ago... ...her in one... hand... ...slowered her... to the floor.

...rising was easier this time...—and walked over to Mara.

HEALTHY, 5'6", 130 LBS.

8 YRS

FIT. ~~CO~~

~~PERFECTION~~

BRUISED. UNCLEAR ON

DIFFERENCE BETWEEN ...

M

MASSIVE EGO. DO NOT LIKE. ~~NO GOOD REASON~~

EVERY REASON.

...should have trusted her instincts.

...If... ...I... ...speak... ...y close enough to get in Mara's face. Your nose is bro...

...pretended to be unconscious

...ruin your...

...s e ll...

...heroin

...and...

a push in the right direction. ...an addict through and through

...the truth behind the mask

every cruel

body   here

disappeared. "We   *find*

Mi

S   s   y

ou   eyes

confesse to   M

There's   corpse

this time.

"Let me unlock your handcuffs

vatively. You run   ly well. Let's see   **run**

Run   You could   the nerve

can't shoot me   you   you

             were

worthy   you

             I   you

I'll walk away

     aside from Kelly's b

'll leave you bound

     tomb

recovered   But he didn't

he hadn't, and that mean

                              At

best, you

           is going to kill you

He's   out there, and he knows who to hunt.

Your cruelty makes you a target to be destroyed.

she feared

the

Snakes

with

barbed wire lips and bared

white teeth.

th e flush of energy
she

experienced

her

worrisome

exterior
burst into

tears.

wrapped

in languages

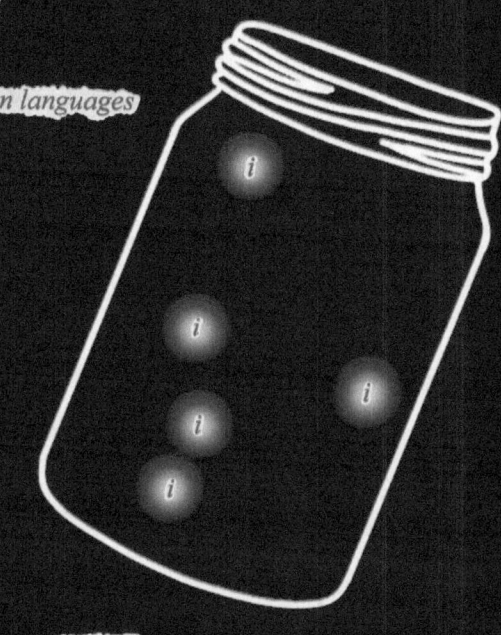

capture

and conceal

rumbling voice s

slid toward unconsciousness,

hidden under

swollen eyes and

terror

trauma

settled on

Her

stripped off   gown

"Why should I believe you?" she

believe you?" she

u   n   s   e

a   m   s

how she had loved

her name

as what he called her.

if you're so cold,

"I don't like to be confined."

I knew that. crowded
corner

she relaxed and allowed

her own t deconstructed image.

to start.

a light dusting of body

mouth dry.

a slow, soft exhale.

She broke

doesn't matter

explore?

think, about the stability and strength of that hand convinced her that thinking

then she knew why. scarred and scared and broken,

a long breath, throw, pulled off her

she got to help her naked then she was naked naked together, and for the first time s... see-ing

safe.

not necessarily happy ...within reason.

She froze,

own fear.

smelled her

ory of her tone grated at him. Annie and Leo would never put up with an insolent driver.

Before the unease blossomed, Carson called in again. "Max, why are people loading Kellen onto an airplane?"

"What are you talking about?"

"They're carrying her up the steps into a corporate jet."

Max found himself on his feet. "Who is? What kind of corporate jet?"

"This woman. This guy in a pilot's uniform. Big jet. She's unconscious."

"Stop them!"

"They carried her inside. They shut the door. The logo on the plane says Lykke Industries. Does that mean anything to you?"

"Yes." Max's heart stopped. This wasn't possible. Not after he'd just found her again. Not when they'd come so close. "It means Kellen is about to die."

45

~~Katlian woke to the drone of an airplane in flight.~~
~~She knew where she was before she opened her eyes.~~
~~Under her nose, she smelled expensive carpet, so she~~
~~was sprawled facedown in the airplane aisle. But some-~~
~~thing close at hand emitted another odor,~~ the reek of
something burned and rotting. The stench ~~made her~~
~~want to~~ vomit.

~~Her fear made her want to cry.~~
~~The truth made her want to hide.~~
~~She remembered everything. Every damned Caci-~~
~~lia thing.~~
~~She wished she didn't. She wished she could forget~~
~~she had never been~~ ~~Katlia,~~ weak, broken and guilty.
~~For years now, she had pretended to be Kollor, to be~~
~~strong, fearless. But here, on the floor of the Lykke In-~~
~~dustries jet, the only thing that seemed real was — she~~
~~was an~~ impostor.
~~She pulled her hands to her chest, used them to lever~~
~~herself up.~~
Everything hurt. ~~Her shattered sternum robbed her of~~

Kellen saw the chink in Erin's devotion, and she pressed her advantage. "You approved of everything he did. You want to approve of me."

Bitterly now, Erin said, "You didn't deserve him."

"That's for sure. No one deserves to be hurt, brutalized, killed. He was a murderer, but you're not. Not yet."

Erin laughed. She laughed, all nasty and amused. "My mother wanted to warn you I was coming for you."

Kellen stood still for a critical moment. "Your mother wanted to warn me?"

"I couldn't let her do that."

"So you . . . killed Sylvia? You killed your mother?"

Erin smacked Kellen with a roundhouse to the jaw.

Kellen dropped to her knees, her head ringing. Every time she inhaled, pain knifed her lungs. Every time she lifted her hand, the swelling intensified.

"I smothered her with a pillow. She was senile, babbling about how she had bred monsters by a monster. She was talking about me and Gregory, and about our father." Erin swayed back and forth like a charmed cobra. "She said she loved us, but she called us monsters."

Kellen cradled her aching jaw and collected bits and pieces of consciousness. She opened her swollen eyes and with her left hand pulled herself to her feet. "Erin Lyleke, you're going to hell."

"No." Erin had the audacity to look hurt. "She deserved it. She was going to betray Gregory." She started toward Kellen.

Kellen backed up, drawing Erin farther into the galley.

Erin laughed. "You're puffing like a freight train gasping its way up a mountain. What good do you think window, peeling away a two-foot-wide chunk of the plane's fuselage from ceiling to floor.

Erin disappeared into the void. The reeking wreck of Gregory's body vanished out the hole with Erin.

The plane rocked out of control.

Kellen careened back and forth, helpless, caught in forces beyond her control. Her injured hand slipped and slipped again. She clutched with her good hand, but . . .

No air.

No gravity.

No strength.

She fought to again grasp the metal leg with her swollen fingertips.

The plane spiraled downward.

She couldn't breathe. She was losing consciousness.

She was going to die.

the eastern sky

mask

ed
every fiber

of her being.

in

blinding pain

  if

                    everything

                                        imagined   had
really been

                                          ...

plain

                              wide sky

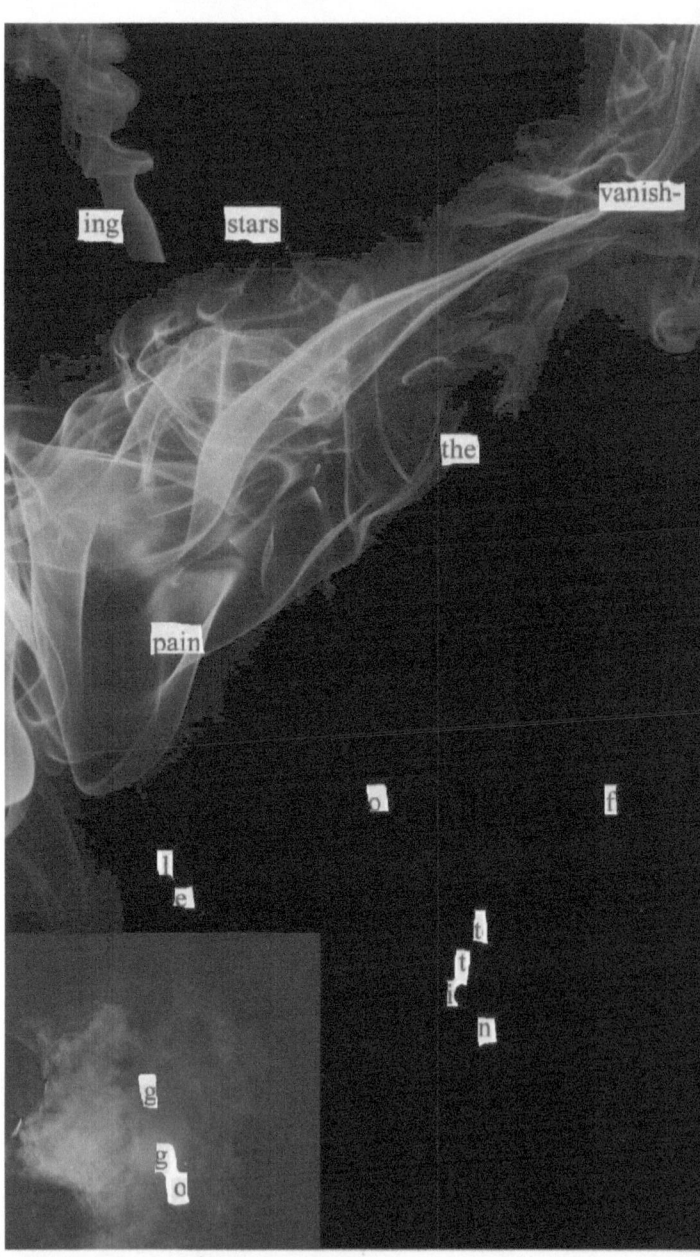

ing   stars   vanish-

                    the

        pain

            o   f

    l
     e

                t
               t
              i
               n

        g

          g
           o

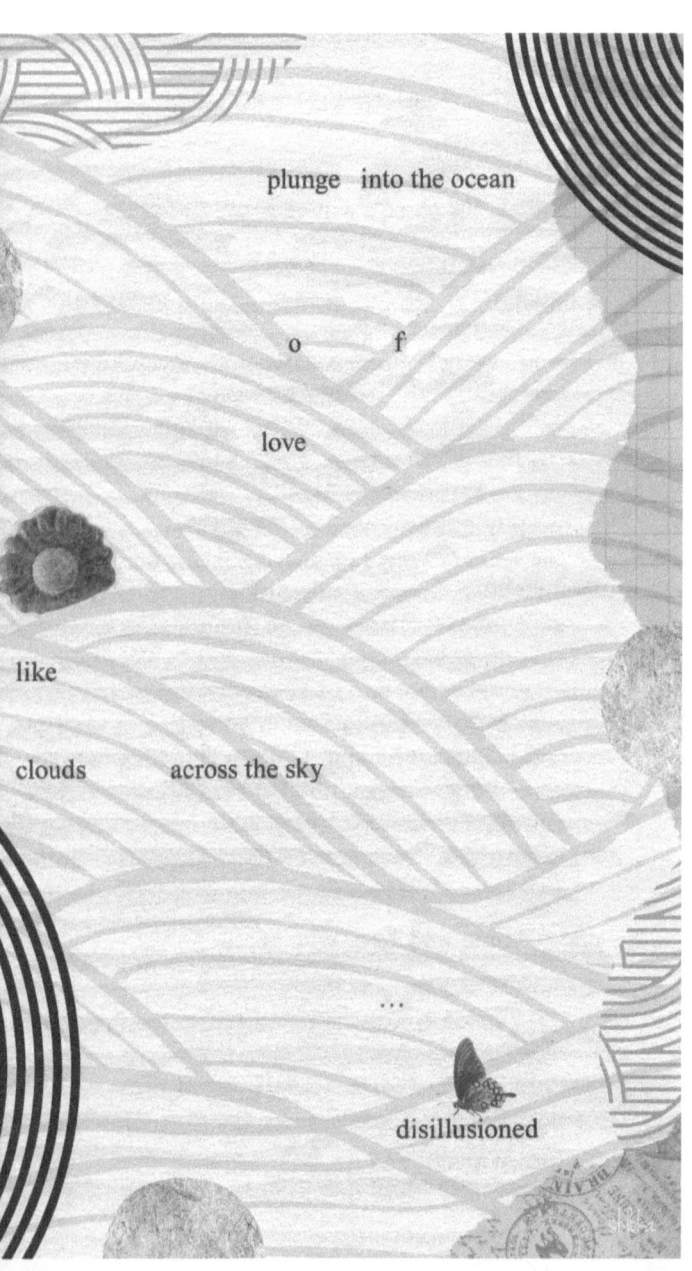

plunge into the ocean

o   f

love

like

clouds   across the sky

. . .

disillusioned

pital had returned Kellen to the most fragile of health, but Kellen didn't care—she was alive. *They* were alive.

Birdie put the car in gear and started toward the resort. **ALIVE ALIVE**

Kellen turned on the seat heater, struggled out of her winter coat and settled back to the road as it wound through groves and over hills toward the resort. "I heard from Nils. **WATCH**

is more than we have," Birdie said in exasperation. "When the government took Mara away, he disappeared in a hurry."

"He's got a job. An important job." All Kellen's doubts had been set at rest. Nils Brooks really was MFAA. "He said she's in custody." **HEAR**

Birdie hesitated. "I hope so. I hope she doesn't escape. I don't know why I think she can but I do, and I'm more afraid of her than I ever was of anyone in Afghanistan." **THINK THINK THINK**

Kellen put her hand on Birdie's shoulder. "I know. I used to think that gleam in her eyes was competitiveness. Now I think it's ego and rabid lunacy." **HEAR**

"Did you hear when the Feds went into her cottage to search for evidence, her bedroom closet was locked, and when they got it open, it was full of books?" Birdie glanced at Kellen. "I mean—books. First editions, autographed editions and part of a genuine Gutenberg Bible. The stash is worth millions." **LOOK**

"She was illiterate and locked her books in a closet. Isn't that symbolic?" **GLANCE**

"And—" Birdie looked vaguely ill.

"What else?"

"Hands. Mummified."

pressed her back against the seat trying to get away from the vision.

a breath

Keller imagine the

ing the resort's commercial-sized dehydrators out the windows. twisted and warped. Does anybody know who she really

BREATHE

appeared out of nowhere."

Like me. the thought corrupted

her claws in him."

swerved as Birdie half turned toward Kel-

I just feel stupid trusting him if I have her to blame."

"He tried to kill us. For money and maybe for sex with her? but he hurt me and he hurt you.
I don't mourn him.

"Okay. You don't have to." As badly as Birdie had been injured, Keller didn't blame her a bit.

Birdie the day after they took Mara away."

tell me more give a damn."

shook her head. "Guess again."

stumbling on the
way

back

my life

in pain

words

feel light

around

ry   o   u

say something

vibrant

Your life is about to change.

h e

helped her out.

not yet thirty,
bandages   and swelling
reshaped her face.
          they stood together,
and   looked so

Strong. Stable.

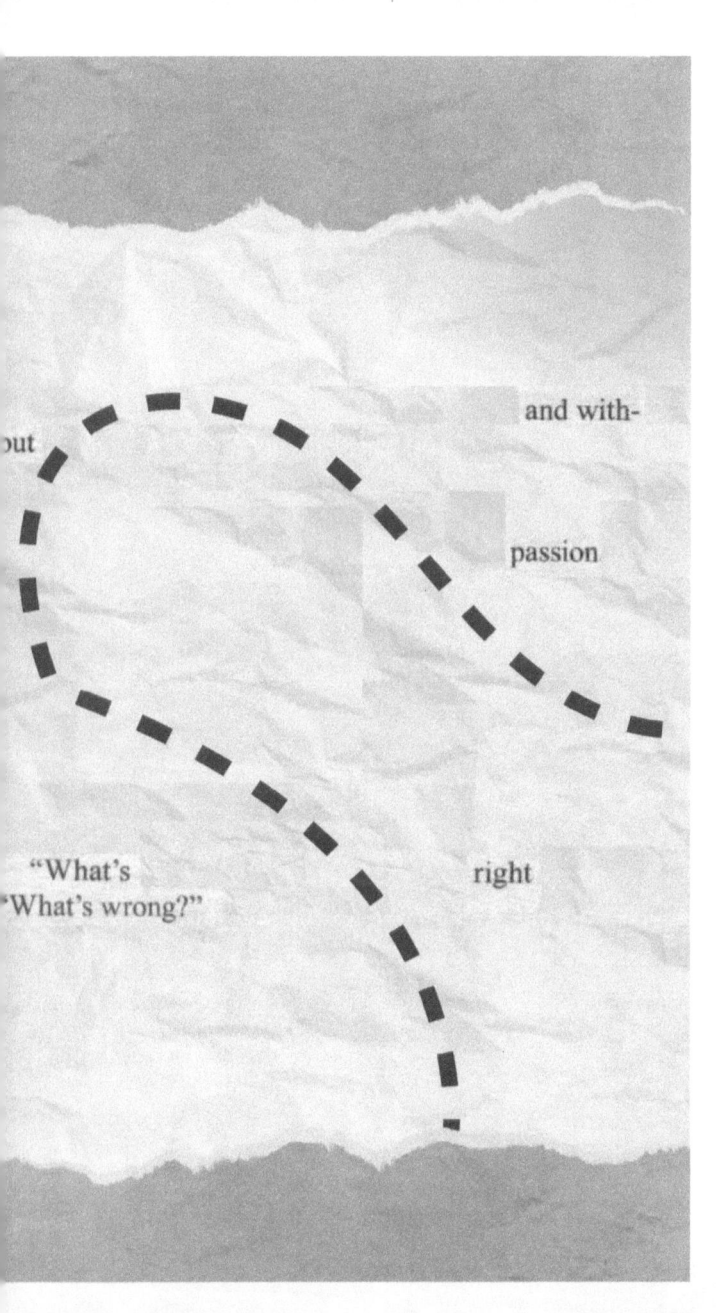

read

her in silence
with interest

f o

r

a few moments

"Leo and I wanted Kellen to know she had support from us," Annie turned her wheelchair and started for the door. "And we do support you, dear, no matter what you decide."

The woman Max called mama stood, also. "She does not need support, Annie. No one here is against her."

Kellen felt like the elephant in the room. But she was so sure she recognized the little girl she couldn't speak.

Had the child been a guest at the resort?

No, Kellen didn't have a profile in her brain.

Leo and Hammett followed Annie, and Leo in a low, masculine conspiratorial voice said to Max. "It was her idea."

Max nodded.

His mother leaned down and spoke to the little girl. To Rae.

Rae stopped hopping and stood very still, arms stiff at her sides, but she beamed at Kellen and Kellen had to smile back.

Max's mother walked toward him but asked repressively, "Are you sure, Maximilian?"

"We need time to get matters cleared up," Max said.

What things? Kellen wanted to ask. *What did they need to clear up? Who was the child?*

Max pushed his relatives out of the room and shut the door behind them.

The profile Kellen was attempting to produce kept getting scrambled by that smile, that excitement, that blond hair, those dimples. "Who is she?" she asked Max.

"You don't know?" His voice sounded as if it was coming up from a deep well.

"I swear I've never seen her before." Kellen chuckled.

reached and thank God I stopped to check for the key or I would have been in the wrong place at the wrong time. A broken piece of terra-cotta tile piercing her hip was better than a six-pound roof tile slamming down on her cranium. She had enough trouble with her head… "I'm going to try to bring him down safely, but get the EMTs here ASAP."

Rita gave a squawk that sounded like, "Whatnotrooffall?"

Kellen guessed they didn't get emergencies like this very often. "Send help!" She hung up.

From above, she heard Roderick yell again. How much had he imbibed that he'd climbed onto the roof of a three-story building and almost fallen to his death? The original estate on this site had been orchards surrounding an early twentieth century farmhouse. A few towering cherry trees surrounded the now remodeled farmhouse and provided gracious shade for the well-tended yard. The trees still bore fruit, and workers now picked the fruit and loaded it into buckets strapped to their belts.

She ran into the trees, each step more and more crooked as the pain in her hip blossomed into agony. A twenty-foot spike ladder leaned against a tree; the picker was all the way up in the top branches. She grabbed the ladder and lifted it. Every muscle in her poor abused hip told her that was a mistake.

In the tree, the picker cursed at her.

"Thank you!" she yelled and headed back to the winery, dragging the long heavy wooden ladder behind her.

The winery building was three stories of classic Tuscan architecture, a jewel that glowed like ancient amber in the setting of Oregon's long lush Willamette Valley.

Also Available From Gnashing Teeth Publishing

Heat the Grease, We're Frying Up Some Poetry (anthology)

Love Notes You'll Never Read (anthology)

Rain Minnows [Notecards and Poems] by Joshua Bridgewater Hamilton

Winter Zine (limited release)

Insurrection (anthology)

malepoet by PW Covington

SHE: Seen. Heard. Engaged. Vol. 1 (anthology)

Meditations & Mediations by Dr. Rebecah Hall

places I never want to see again by Keriann Gilson

Sleep Cinematic or A Golem's Quartet by Les Epstein

Lunafly by Raymond Luczak

Stepping on Legos (limited release zine)

Ghostword by Crisosto Apache

When I Wear Bob Kaufman's Eyes by Tom Murphy

Get Me Out of Here and Other Plays by Pete Lutz

Lorenzo by the Ghost Light by Les Epstein

Fuck Me: A Memoir by L Scully

Spurned (limited release zine)

Moonlight and Monsters by Lauren Scharhag

Finally: The Mixtape by Asela Lee Kemper

A Dangerous Heaven by Jo Angela Edwins

Shared Blood by Luke Wortley

La Santa Madre Tamalera by Juan Perez

the catastrophe of after: a short stay diary by Emily Kay MacGriff

Support Independent Presses

Ask For Our Books to Be Stocked at Your Local Bookseller

http://GnashingTeethPublishing.com

GNASHING TEETH

PUBLISHING

words that get in your teeth